D1827471

Procrastinating

Self Help Guide to Implementing Six Sigma
Strategies to Your Startup, Make More Money in
Your Small Business

(Time Management Secrets to Supercharge Your
Productivity)

Dan Rock

Published by Kevin Dennis

© **Dan Rock**

All Rights Reserved

ISBN 978-1-989965-01-6

Legal & Disclaimer

The information contained in this book is not designed to replace or take the place of any form of medicine or professional medical advice. The information in this book has been provided for educational and entertainment purposes only.

The information contained in this book has been compiled from sources deemed reliable, and it is accurate to the best of the Author's knowledge; however, the Author cannot guarantee its accuracy and validity and cannot be held liable for any errors or omissions. Changes are periodically made to this book. You must consult your doctor or get professional medical advice before using any of the

Table of Contents

Introduction

In today's busy world, it can often feel like there's too much to be done in too little time. Using time efficiently is imperative to completing tasks on time and leaving yourself enough hours at the end of the day to spend with your family, or doing the things that matter to you. To use your time wisely, however, requires focus, efficiency, and continuous productivity. If you're someone that finds it difficult to keep thinking about the task at hand, or a chronic procrastinator, it can often seem like there are even fewer hours in the day.

Luckily, focus and productivity are skills, and like any skill, they can be learned and practiced. Whether you struggle with procrastination or simply want to find a way to manage your time more efficiently, the information and skills that follow in these chapters will help you to make the most of your work day. The first two chapters focus on ways you can improve your brain's thinking power and set up your physical work space for success. The last three explore multitasking, motivation, and procrastination, looking at ways you can change your habits and develop the discipline to get the most out of your days.

Chapter 1: Laziness And Procrastination

Does This Sound Familiar?

Let's say your boss assigns you an important task or project that needs to be completed in one month. To make things even more interesting, let's assume this project is neither interesting and engaging, nor annoying and challenging. It's simply the kind of job that you can quickly complete without having to invest an enormous amount of motivation and effort. All you know for sure is that it's important and has to be completed within one month. Otherwise, heads will roll.

It has been four or five days since you received the project and you already have a few ideas on how you're going to tackle it. That's good, right!? I mean, in a sense, you already have a plan. Not a carefully drawn plan with step-by-step instructions, reasonable milestones and clear deadlines, but nonetheless, a plan. Considering that you already know how this whole thing will evolve, you probably feel calm and relieved. Plus, you have twenty-five more days, so no worries.

Let's say it's Friday, and since there are only twenty days left until the due date, you decide to spend your entire weekend working on this big project. It's 8 pm and the phone suddenly rings. It's one of your friends, calling to invite you out for drinks. Since it's Friday and you've worked your butt off this whole week, a night out with a couple of good friends is just what you deserve. Plus, tomorrow is Saturday, so you'll have plenty of time to take care of that important project.

Your Friday night out lasted until 5 am and as a result, you've slept through all of Saturday. But after you get out of bed, around noon, you pour yourself a cup of coffee and start working on that project you've been putting off for ten days now.

Although you have fifteen more days 'til the big day and you haven't even completed 1/4 of the project, things don't seem to be that bad. In the last week or so, you've managed to work on your big project almost on a daily basis. If you push a little bit harder, you'll finish on time.

Ten more days until due date and you still haven't reached 50%. At this point, anxiety kicks in, and you have a sudden boost in motivation which skyrockets your productivity. But that doesn't last for long because, just like the rest of us, you need to take a break and recharge your batteries.

About a week 'til due date and you decide that now's the time to make this project your number one priority. You sit at your desk, put your smartphone away and focus entirely on the job at hand. After a while, you take a short lunch break. You look around the house and, all of a sudden you remember all the house chores that needed to be done a long time ago. **Maybe I should put the project on hold for an hour or so and wash this huge pile of dirty dishes.** After all, it's not like you're having fun. You're just trying to squeeze this "important" task into your already busy schedule. After you're finished with the dishes, you then move to dusting, taking out the trash, washing the windows, folding the clothes, changing the sheets, mopping the floors and fixing that broken bicycle chain you've been putting off for months.

Three days left and you're like "holy sh*t." **Right now, the situation is starting to feel tense.** Will I be able to finish on time? What if I don't sleep? Then I'll have more time to work on my project. What could happen if I don't finish this on time? Maybe I can come up with a good explanation, and my boss won't fire me? **That is the bargaining part; the moment when panic sets in and our productivity goes down the drain.**

This "tragic" story can end in two ways. Either you push yourself to the limit and manage to pull this off on time, but at a lower quality and with almost zero energy left for other tasks, or you simply give up and brace yourself for the torrent of criticism that awaits you on the due date.

As you can see, procrastination is a silent killer, starting with some innocent postponing and ending with you jumping through hoops to complete impossible tasks. So how can we avoid such unpleasant scenarios? How can we nip procrastination in the bud and prevent it from unleashing this terrible chain of events that ruins our productivity and leads to less than mediocre performances?

Procrastination is more than laziness

You might be inclined to think "**That's not me. The guy you're describing is lazy and ignorant.**" In a sense, you're right. From the outside, procrastination and laziness look very alike. In both cases, people tend to postpone important tasks or projects repeatedly. Also, both practices affect productivity as well as other relevant aspects of everyday life.

However, the reason behind our behavior is what makes the difference between procrastination and laziness. While a lazy person might say "**I don't want to do it,**" someone who's struggling with procrastination will probably say "**I'll do it later.**" To put it differently, procrastinators do intend to assume responsibility and work on their tasks, but for some reason, something always seems to mess up their schedule. On the other hand, people who are lazy don't even have a schedule. They avoid responsibilities and don't have the slightest intention of doing something productive, not even for themselves, let alone for those who might need their help. Laziness or "couch potato" syndrome is a state of lethargy (with no apparent cause) characterized by daydreaming, lack of motivation and energy, and a profound sense of hopelessness. Although laziness lacks the scientific basis to qualify as a diagnosable condition, experts agree this problem should be treated with the same seriousness as any other physical or mental condition.

Lazy people spend most of the day in bed, watching TV or playing on their smartphones. To put it differently, they enjoy being in a constant state of idleness and will continue to perpetuate this state for as long as the circumstances allow them. Gradually, they become addicted to their carefree lifestyle which seems to bring tons of benefits (at least for the time being). Both scientists and mental health professionals warn that, in time, such counterproductive behaviors can result in depression, relationships issues, obesity, arthritis and much more.

As for procrastination, this behavior is defined as the unjustified postponement of an important task, project or activity despite the negative consequences that may arise from our inability to follow through with the initial plan. Procrastination might also be the reason why we leave an important decision until the last minute.

People who procrastinate often "rationalize" their decision and eliminate the shame or guilt associated with their counterproductive behavior by engaging in other less important activities. To put it differently, you'll probably see them cleaning the house or taking care of errands right before a big exam.

But that's not the only "strategy" procrastinators use to deflect attention from the obvious irrationality of their constant delays. Sometimes, they say they're more tired than they are, or find all sorts of "logical" explanations as to why a certain task or project is not that urgent.

Although the number of people who do not procrastinate at all is close to zero, the seriousness of this behavior is linked to the degree to which its negative consequences affect us.

As you can see, it's relatively easy to confuse procrastination with laziness. Both conditions seem to have the same effect on our productivity, and neither is classified as a psychological problem.

However, while lazy people don't go out of their way to hide their idleness (on the contrary, most of them will gladly admit they're lazy), procrastinators tend to be somewhat sneaky. In a sense, we could argue that while laziness is a conscious and deliberate act, procrastination tends to operate at a subconscious level, making you think you are a relatively productive member of society.

Now that we know the similarities and differences between laziness and procrastination, it's time to unravel the mysteries of this condition by exploring its origins and inner workings.

Chapter 2: Myths And Truths About

Procrastination

A lot of ideas always plague your mind when it comes to procrastination as a topic. While you might enjoy knowing that you aren't the only one doing it, there are also things about it that you should take seriously. Yes, you could research about procrastination but care must be exercised when it comes to separating myths from truths. These things almost go hand in hand and knowing which is which could be quite complicated.

Procrastination myths can take the form of those things that you tell yourself when a task to be done appears. The ones which have been identified by experts are as follows:

Myth #1: Procrastination is normal and sometimes it can be good for us. This myth is obviously capitalizing on the fact that humans are not perfect. For those who believe in this myth, postponing things is a privilege that they think they can abuse. It is good for them because they believe that it could give them a chance to relax and "regroup" for better performance later on.

Myth #2: Procrastination gives you a shot at being a better time manager. This is because when you are rushing to beat a shorter deadline or a deadline extension, you tend to focus more on effective time management. This is an obvious misinterpretation of the idea of time management. Are you really managing time better? Of course, the answer here is no! You are cramming and this is nowhere near the description of perfectly managed time!

Myth #3: Procrastination trains you to work better under pressure. This myth is closely related to #2 as you can see. However, this one has gained more acceptances due to the fact that there are people who can do really well under pressure. What most of us don't realize is that this doesn't apply to all of us. The sheer pressure of short deadlines or time extensions can break people and affect the quality of their work. There are other effective ways to train on performing efficiently and effectively under pressure. One thing is for sure and it's that procrastination isn't one of these.

Myth #4: The need for procrastination is an indication that your current motivation level doesn't yet match the task on hand.

Those who believe in this myth often say that they need more time or inspiration to work on a task. The truth here is that no one needs such things to do their work. The mere fact that the task today will still remain a task tomorrow should already give you an idea that postponing the task is useless. You have the power to set the motivation for the task. It could be as simple as the pleasure of finishing ahead of others.

Myth #5: It is easy to recover from procrastination.

People who believe this will deviate from their work from time to time. They will say that they will just take a peek at the updates on their Facebook page, see what's in their email, or just take a power nap and then go back to work. Can you guess what happens next? Indeed, they will take more time doing those things and end up with piles of work to be done! One hard truth that must be understood is that once procrastination creeps in, it is hard to get out of it. Checking your mail might take just a minute but once some interesting things turn up, it will be difficult to go back to work.

Based on the myths presented above, it is really easy to fall under the illusion that procrastination is something that can be taken lightly. However, it can ruin your life if you will not do something about it. Now, how can it specifically do this? Consider the following:

Time will be lost.

Opportunities will pass you by.

Life goals will not be achieved.

Careers will be ruined.

Self-esteem can go down.

Decisions will be made poorly.

Your reputation will be at a great risk.

Stress-related health problems will set in.

With myths and truths about procrastination finally revealed, you have just gained a better insight on why you must work towards getting it out of your life. Now, the first step in doing this can be found in the next chapter. Go on and discover more!

Chapter 3: Good Habits And Productivity–

The Relation

Your habits define you. The person you are and the lifestyle you are now living is all because of your habits. If you are productive and successful, feel free to thank your healthy, constructive, and good habits. On the other hand, if you are unproductive, lazy, inefficient, and unsuccessful, even then, feel free to blame your bad habits and yourself for building them.

What the above means is that if you want to be extremely productive and achieve your goals, you need to maintain a lifestyle where good habits are your mainstay.

The Big Issue

The problem with most of us is that we cannot understand our daily routine. If this sounds familiar, it is because you are not the only one suffering from this dilemma: many of us are.

There must have been days where you wanted to be extra-productive and get everything done but you ended up doing nothing because one thing or the other kept coming up. This, the manifestation of seemingly urgent things in an otherwise planned schedule is something we are going to discuss in later chapters of this book.

In later chapter, we shall look at how you can free yourself from the cycle of bad habits. Before we get to that, let us discuss how building good habits and breaking your bad ones helps you achieve your goals.

How Changing Your Habits Helps You Become More Productive and Successful

If you do not habitually complete tasks on time, the likelihood is that you procrastinate a lot. If you are not in the habit of focusing on one task at a time and instead, multitask all the time, every likelihood is that you seldom complete all your tasks or execute a task successfully. On the other hand, if your habits are the opposite of this and you do focus on one task at a time, complete a task on its given time, and make sure you manage your distractions while working, you are likely to be quite productive.

This proves that the habits you nurture directly affect your productivity and how fast or slowly you achieve your goals. If you do not make it a point to work towards your goals and regularly do small things that move you towards your aim, you will never accomplish your goals because the things you do repeatedly turn into your habits and when your habits are unhealthy, you will not achieve your desired goals.

To be productive, effective, alert, focused, disciplined, and successful, you MUST build good habits that replace your current unhealthy ones. If you want to build an empowered life, do things your way, achieve everything you set your eyes on, do not want to settle for mediocre things, and want to fulfill all your genuine desires, you have to change your existing negative and unproductive habits into positive and successful ones. If you fail to do, you will not acquire the discipline, power, strength, positivity, and focus you need to manifest your desires and create the life you truly want to live.

With that understanding, let us delve deeper and learn how you can get closer to your success destination simply by making some lifestyle changes.

Chapter 4: Habit Formation: How Habits

Form And Work

As stated earlier, habits are repeated decisions and behavior. Habit formation is the process by which these decisions and behaviors become automatic.

Habits permeate every area of our lives. Unfortunately, because many of the habits that make up our lives are repeated behaviors, we are oblivious of how these automatic behaviors affect our lives. For instance, the first thing many of us do in the morning is stretching a hand out of the warm covers to snooze the alarm we set the previous night. Unknown to us, other than ruining our plans for the day, in terms of how we use our time, this habit also does something equally lethal: it erodes our self-discipline. This erosion is covert, which is why so many of us are unaware of the habits that are ruining our lives.

Habits are the mechanisms the brain uses to enhance its productivity and ability to handle the many stimuli it has to process.

In the pursuit of efficiency, the brain seeks to automate as many behaviors as possible so that when they become habitual, it has more computing power to compute new challenges as they arise.

This mechanism has many benefits; in the same light, it also has its fair share of drawbacks because when the behaviors it automate and makes habitual are negative ones, ones that cast a negative effect on your mind, the results are hard-to-break negative behaviors that take away from your life instead of adding something meaningful to it.

The Formation of Habits and how they Work

Habits, good or bad, form through the same working modalities: they form through, as Charles Duhigg, bestselling author of the book Power of Habits: Why We Do What We Do in Life and Business, this habits book puts it, "a psychological pattern called a **habit loop**."

To understand the habit loop that makes all habits, we need to understand how the mind works:

As we start making a conscious decision to engage in a new task (assume you want to make a conscious decision to work out at a specific time each day) before the brain understands that you are making this decision repeatedly and it should therefore create neuropathways to automate this behavior/decision, it uses a lot of processing power. As hinted at earlier, this power manifests as will and motivation.

In the exercise example above, to get started, to get out of bed instead of snoozing your alarm, wear your boots and running clothes and head out for a run, you will need to WILL yourself out of bed, which will require motivation. As you make this decision countless times and consistently engage in the behavior, the brain starts understanding the intricacies of how the behavior or decision works. When this happens, the brain reduces the mental power it uses to complete that decision and starts looking for ways to automate various parts of the behavior/decision.

A simpler way to understand this is to think back to the immense concentration and focus you had to use as you learnt how to cycle, tie a tie, or even parallel park for the first time, and then compare this to the focus you use to complete these tasks now that you have done them repeatedly.

To turn repeated decisions or behavior into an automated routine, the brain uses a technique Duhigg calls chunking, which means the brain breaks the decisions or behavior into a sequence of actions. Therefore, our daily lives are full of behavioral chunks.

As we indicated earlier, all habits form through a psychological pattern we called the habit loop. The habit loop has three components: the **cue/trigger**, the **routine**, and the **reward**. This loop pattern is the glue that holds together all habits. Therefore, to break a bad habit or even develop a good one, you need to hack this loop, what Duhigg calls the 3rs of habit formation. To do so, you need to understand each of these elements:

The Cue/Reminder

The Cue or reminder is the thing that reminds you to make a certain decision or engage in a certain behavior. Every behavior has a cue or reminder; while some of these cues may be psychological, they exist.

As an example of this, think of what you do before you complete a behavior such as brushing your teeth or getting out of the house. In the first example, you grab your toothbrush; in this, grabbing your toothbrush is the cue (however a behavior—one such as brushing your teeth—can have many cues). In the latter case, grabbing the door handle can be the cue that precipitates the behavior.

As stated, reminders/cues can take many forms: they can be mental, a sound reminder such as an alarm, or even something as mundane as the sight of something or a specific time. For instance, in a work environment, 10 a.m. signals tea break and the behaviors that come with it, while in a school setting, a bell signals specific behaviors.

The reminder is the first habit formation step; without which, habits would not form. Imagine an instance where nothing reminds you to wake up at a specific time or work out. Would this be conducive to repeated decision making? NO.

To break a bad habit, you have to determine its reminder; we shall discuss this in detail as we discuss the habits you need to adopt to achieve success:

The Routine

The routine is the behavior prompted by the cue. In the habit formation process, i.e. to replace bad habits with good ones, you have to tweak the routine. Routines make up your daily life even when you are unaware of their existence. These routines are ones you have formed from repeating certain behaviors.

The brain loves routine because a routine requires very little brainpower, something the mind is always trying to do. To change old habits and create new ones, you need to change up the routine.

Going with the earlier example, brushing your teeth, going out of the house, or heading to your next class or for lunch when the relevant bell rings are the routines prompted by specific cues.

At first, changing the routine will require a lot of mental effort and continued commitment on your part. For instance, if when 10 a.m. beckons (the cue) instead of going to the cafeteria, you want to adopt the positive habit of going out for a short walk in the sunshine, you have to be deliberate and consistent with the routine you practice immediately after the cue. This is how you will turn the new behavior into a routine thereby overwriting the previous bad habit.

The Reward

The reward is the benefit the brain/body gets from completing the behavior. The reward serves the purpose of reinforcing the behavior. As an example, consider an instance where to lose weight, you decide to jog first thing in the morning. The cue could be an alarm, running is the routine, and losing weight is the reward that enforces the behavior. If after changing your routine (perhaps you used to snooze your alarm and now, you get out of bed and get ready to go for your run), you receive the reward, which in this case, is losing weight, the reward shall cement the behavior and you will find yourself working out more so you can enjoy the reward.

Self-interest is the driving force behind everything you do. The bad habits you have adopted offer you some form of reward. For instance, you over-eat comfort foods because they offer you a sense of comfort; you abuse alcohol because it helps you (probably) forget your problems for a while. To change a habit, you will have to find a positive reward for it; this will require a lot of experimentation.

Research from neuroscientists has shown that the basal ganglia is the part of the brain responsible for pattern recognitions, memories, emotions, and more importantly, reward-based learning. On the hand, making decisions on a conscious level uses the prefrontal cortex, the part of your brain responsible for conscious decision-making.

When a behavior becomes automatic, use of the basal ganglia reduces and the brain starts working less. Duhigg puts it as follows, **"The brain can almost completely shut down. ... And this is a real advantage, because it means you have all of this mental activity you can devote to something else."** Decreased use of the basal ganglia is why as you peddle, you can focus on other things such as the scenery of the song blasting over your headphones.

Duhigg then says, "You can complete complex behaviors without mental awareness thanks to the capacity of our basal ganglia to take a behavior and turn it into an automatic routine."

We now understand how habits form and work, let us now discuss another habit formation theory and thereafter look at a detailed, systematic process you can use to create good habits that overwrite bad ones.

Chapter 5: Take A Break!

When you work for extended periods of time on a project, you become subject to a phenomenon we like to call "burn out"! What this means is that your mind becomes mentally exhausted and is unable to process any more information. When we're working, we don't want this!

The best way to get your brain to start coming back from its hibernation is to TAKE A BREAK! This will rejuvenate your brain cells and get your blood pumping. What I mean by "taking a break" is to find an activity that does not involve your current line of work. It can be any sort of activity at all, but make sure to follow the following guidelines.

When you're taking a break, make sure to do something that has nothing to do with what you're working on, so that you can "clear your head". You can do many different things with your time, so it gets a little mind boggling to think about your options. Instead, just do your best to get your head out of the clouds and on to something else.

The amount of time that you should take your break should be around 15-60 minutes in length. Any longer and you may not want to get back to work! The goal here is just to get your mental gears moving in the right direction, not give yourself an excuse to do a time-consuming activity.

It was Leonardi Da Vinci who figured out that we need one hour of sleep for every three hours that we're awake. If you take this into consideration, then you can do the same regarding your work. Of course, back in those days, he was able to work throughout the day and take quick naps as he pleased. Nowadays, not all of us have that leisure.

Current psychological studies have shown that the average attention span of a normal human being sitting down and focusing on a topic is about 50 minutes. Take into consideration that most college courses only last for about 50 minutes (minus laboratory courses or extended classes) and you can see just how these studies are used in our daily lives.

To make the most of your productivity when you're sitting down for a project that does not require physical work (such as sitting in front of the computer, studying, reading a book, knitting, etc.), then try working for 50 minutes at a time with 15 minute intermissions.

NOTE: this does not work for everyone, so if it doesn't work for you, then try some of the other tips that I have in this book.

Chapter 6: Understanding Procrastination
It seems so simple to set a goal for the week knowing you have seven days to tackle it. But just when you decide to act on it, something distracts you. It could be a text message, a phone call, sudden hunger pangs, that pile of clutter you've been meaning to clean up for the past month or just the realization that you don't want to do it considering you still have six other days to complete it. The list of possible distractions is endless. Before you know it, you're left with a minimal amount of time and either doing a subpar job or finishing it later than planned.

Understanding why people procrastinate can help both you and the people affected by your procrastination see it in a different light. Although psychologists have disagreed about the reasons for procrastination, the common belief today is that procrastinators lack the qualities that help them bridge the gap between intention and action. Those qualities include time management, self-regulation, and learning strategies.

Three studies by University of Bible land (Germany) psychologists Axel Grund and Stefan Fries may help people better understand procrastination. They considered the opinion that procrastination is not only the failure to follow through with one's intentions but not expecting the intention to be completed on time in the first place. In other words, people who don't do things on time don't value the same goals as their counterparts. Grund and Fries went on to say that they understood that procrastination reflects one's difficulties in pursuing goals but that it is also important to understand the person's values. In other words, think of it from the person's point of view. Perhaps they don't see the behavior of procrastination as a form of weakness or misconduct. Instead, maybe they place a higher value on things like well-being and tolerance. If the person values their well-being more than they value timeliness, they may focus more on avoiding any stress that they associate with the task.

Study #1

To prove their theory that procrastination is less of personal weakness and more of a situational occurrence associated with values, they studied the values of people who claimed to be procrastinators. The goal was to answer the question: Would these self-proclaimed procrastinators value their well-being (such as enjoying their free time) more than they value achieving a goal?

Using a sample of 223 undergraduates, the psychologists looked at their study habits and their personal lives. When the students didn't feel a connection to their homework, they tended to do other things with their time. As a result, the psychologists were able to prove their theory, that procrastination is directly related to a person's sense of well-being and the way they value personal enjoyment. Grund and Fries were further able to conclude that procrastination reflects a mismatch between basic motivational structures and current engagement.

Study #2

In the second study in their series, Grund and Fries asked a similar sample of undergrads to use a diary to report on five tasks that they'd planned to complete every day for seven consecutive days. Besides being expected to answer questions related to whether or not they'd completed the tasks, the participants were also expected to rate the extent that they planned to do the activity, according to whether they wanted to do the task or whether the task was only to comply with an eternal set of expectations.

The idea of answering the question about who expected the task — themselves or an external source — was important to the researchers because they believed that procrastinators were more likely to procrastinate when the tasks were assigned by someone else, opposed to when the tasks were self-assigned because they felt connected to them on a personal level. What the psychologists found, as expected, was that the activities that were completed were the ones that participants felt they had more control over and were self-assigned.

Study #3

In the third and final study, Grund and Fries examined the belief in the Protestant work ethic (which claims that people spend too much time in unprofitable amusements) as an influence on the way people perceive unhurried behavior. The researchers asked participants to read a scenario describing the story of a student who intended to study over the weekend for an exam, but who instead spent time with friends. After reading the story, the participants were asked to rate the extent of the student's lack of self-discipline in the story (a trait interpretation) versus whether it was more because the student hadn't recently spent enough time with friends (situational).

They also indicated whether they aligned themselves more with conservatism (the importance of having a belief system), humanitarian-egalitarian values (the importance of being kind to everyone) or having a Protestant work ethic. Finally, they were asked to rate themselves on their general tendency to procrastinate. Again, the findings supported the psychologists' prediction that people who held conservative values and had a Protestant work ethic considered procrastination to reflect a personal, moral failure.

The use of undergraduates as participants of the study was significant because of the idea that young adults sometimes feel like they don't have much control over their time while in college. They may procrastinate when their assigned tasks don't have inherent meaning to them.

What to Do With This Newfound Understanding

Although not everyone agrees, Grund and Fries believe that attempting to force procrastinators to complete tasks on time will be more harmful than beneficial. Instead, they recommend promoting what they call "motivational competence," as a more effective method. Doing so lets people choose and set their own goals — goals that are more in line with their inner values and motives. This applies to the workplace too, not just college. When employees feel connected to their careers, they're more committed to their employer and deliver better work on time.

In conclusion, Getting rid of the idea that procrastination is a negative trait can help develop a better understanding of it. If you consider yourself to be a procrastinator, try not to see yourself in a negative light. Instead, take a broader approach to the understanding of how your values may influence your desire to get things done. Try to connect yourself to the task at hand to make it more valuable to you personally. There is more on that later in this book.

Chapter 7: Getting To Grips With

Mornings

The first thing that you need to do is to reset your body clock. At the moment, it is accustomed to getting up at a set time in the morning. Set your clock one and a half hours earlier than you usually get up.

You need to change the way that you view life, and that includes going to bed earlier than usual and getting a full night's sleep, waking in the morning with plenty of time on your hands to be able to approach your day with a very proactive mind, rather than taking it for granted that you are just there because it's morning.

Breathing in the Air of the Morning

If you do have a back yard, make your first stop to go out into the yard to breathe in fresh air. If you don't, then open your bedroom window and stand in front of it. Over the course of the night, your body has become sleepy and that's natural, but what wakes you up and sharpens your mind is to breathe in the fresh air and to allow it to help your sympathetic nervous system to distribute that oxygen to all the necessary parts of your body.

What you may not know is that most people only use 5 percent of their lung capacity. This restricts the flow of oxygen to all of the right places. We breathe in a very shallow manner. This time, stand with your back straight and breathe in through the nostrils. The nostrils have filters that block out the kind of toxins that our cities are full of and they also serve another purpose. They make the air the right temperature for it to be used correctly by the body.

Breathe in to the count of 8 and feel that air going into your upper gut.

Hold the breath inside for the count of 5

Then breathe out to the count of 10.

Do this half a dozen times because it's waking you up in the most natural way that you can be woken up and after a night of bodily healing, which happens while you sleep, this is a wonderful way to feel alive and ready for the other routines that you are about to introduce into your mornings.

The first few mornings that you introduce this new routine, you will begin to see a difference, but when you do it every single morning, you will miss the fresh air if you miss this part of the routine out at any time. It's a great routine to have wherever you are and whatever you are doing because of the internal effects of correct breathing. In fact, next to drinking water, how you breathe is probably high on the list of changes you need to make in your life.

The optimism that you feel for the day that lies ahead starts with that first breath of fresh air. You will find that the more you are able to commune with nature, the happier you will feel. Thus, it's important to know the value of fresh air and how it can make you feel alive first thing in the morning.

Meditation

You may have heard people mention that they meditate and not have taken much notice of what this involves. Believe me, anyone is capable of doing it and you will need at least 20 minutes each morning to make the most of the practice as a routine. This after you have taken in the air, this is the ideal time to get down to meditation. Before you do, make sure that you have had your morning constitutional and that you are not likely to be in need of the toilet before the end of your meditation session.

I usually use a glass of water as a refreshing drink before I meditate, but you should never eat before meditation. Thus, don't be tempted to grab your breakfast before you settle down to your meditation session in the morning. If you really want a nice taste in your mouth, add the zest of a lemon to the water as that helps to clean out your system and leaves you will a wonderful clean sensation in your mouth, before you even perform your ablutions and clean your teeth.

For meditation, you will need to have a solid chair, such as dining chair. If you go into meditation in a big way later on, you may want to invest in a yoga mat, but for the moment, you don't have to be that formal. You also need to be in comfortable clothing so your pajamas will be super.

Sit with your back straight and make sure that your bare feet at flat on the floor. This helps in grounding you and that's important when you meditate. Place one hand on your lap, palm facing upward and place the other in it, in a similar pose with your thumbs touching each other.

The idea of meditation is to concentrate solely on your breathing and nothing else. When other thoughts come into your mind, imagine them to be pictures on a TV screen that come and then let go of them. Do not attach any other thoughts to the thoughts that come to you. Simply view them, acknowledge them and then let them go and go back to your breathing exercises.

Breathe in through the nostrils to the count of 7

Hold the breath for the count of three

Breathe out to the count of ten.

Count the number one.

These three breathing motions count as one exercise. Thus, each time you complete the three motions you count one, though to ten. It's unlikely that you will get to ten without thoughts imposing so don't beat yourself up if this happen. Simple move on and start the counting back at one again.

You will find that you feel calmer when you meditate. You do need to find a place where you can be on your own and if you want to create a space that's just for meditation, then some people find it helpful to have some kind of altar or area that gives them the inspiration to meditate.

You can find all kinds of inspirational objects that you can place into that room, such as Buddha statue or a diffuser for essential oils or anything that you find will help you to keep to the habit of meditating every single day.

Why Meditation Helps

It helps for a specific reason. You become more comfortable with your thoughts and your body and mind are able to work in harmony. You will find that your concentration levels increase and that while you are meditating, your heartbeat and your blood pressure go down. This helps you to appreciate the calm in your life, which will help you to cope with all of the things that are thrown at you during the day.

After meditation, simply take your time to get up and start your day, but before you do that, write in a diary what you believe you can do better next time in your meditation because this gives your heartbeat and your blood pressure a moment to normalize before going on to your next routine.

Meditation during the day

When you meditate on a regular basis what you are doing is allowing your mind to feel totally at ease with your body. You find that it calms you and helps your clarity. Thus you can use it when faced with stressful situations. It's a wonderful way of letting go of self-doubt and embracing your spirituality.

There are several ways that you can incorporate this into your day and one of the most effective is walking meditation. If you know that you have a heavy workload ahead and want to get into the right state of mind, you simply choose a peaceful place and, as you walk, you concentrate solely on your breathing and the movement of your feet against the floor.

Think of your senses, rather than anything else because if you let thoughts get into your mind, that's not true meditation. When you learn what meditation is all about, you let go of thoughts and are able to see things from a much clearer perspective.

If you think of the mind as being a series of boxes where all your thoughts go into different categories, while you are meditating, you close those boxes and allow your mind to simply concentrate on those things that are relevant to the meditation. That frees you from worry. It frees you from automatic assumptions that things will go wrong and it makes your footsteps into your life much surer.

Thus, it's great to meditate before an interview. You can also use it ahead of meetings with difficult clients. The problem with these situations is that the first word that goes through your mind is DIFFICULT. Put all of that out of your mind and you approach the meeting with a much more positive viewpoint and may actually find that the disagreeable client isn't as disagreeable as you first supposed.

We make up these scenarios in our heads and if you approach what you see as a disagreeable person, your approach will always be negative and have negative results. However, if you meditate and let all of those negative thoughts go, you approach with a much better state of mind and are able to tame even the most difficult of people.

Meditation can also be used for inspiration and I will show you how this can be done in the chapter relating to inspiration. If you are inspired, that means that you have something to look forward to and that's very important in life. Those who are uninspired don't put their best foot forward and seem to go into life half-heartedly. How can you expect great results if you treat life as the enemy? Start to meditate and get those negative thoughts out of your mind. If you do this on a daily basis it helps to keep all of those negative thoughts carefully boxed up so that they do not get in the way of productivity and happiness.

When you expect a child to lie to you, they will invariably do that. When you meditate, you are more capable of accepting people for who they are and children are less likely to keep you out of the picture. With all of the stresses that we are exposed to on almost a daily basis, it's hardly any wonder that people go into their working day with a sense of dread. By taking the stance of meditating daily, you lift your spirit and find your purpose in life and that's extremely important. We all need to feel that we have some reason to keep on doing what we are doing and meditation makes that reason very clear indeed and helps us to see our work as a simple small part of our existence, rather than letting work become who we are.

Chapter 8: The Reason Tasks Take Longer

You can dramatically reduce the time it takes to complete tasks. You can do this by doing just one thing. You won't be using a calender planner any more.

When people complete a task, the first thing they do is think about what to do first and how to do it. As they go along, they continue this process. Quite often, they'll stop to think of a better way of doing it. All of these things extend the time it takes. The problem is the thinking time.

How much faster would you complete your task, if you took away all the thinking?

How to remove the thinking

In a word, it's planning. Do all the thinking beforehand. By doing this no thinking will be required during the task. All you'll have to do, is sit down and do it. You will already know the best way, what to do, and when to do it. No thinking needed.

Here's an example to show what I'm getting at...

Years ago, I used to go to a local gym. I trained hard. I'd spend an hour and a half to two hours five days a week.

When I went in, I would look around and decide what exercise I would do first. After, I would think about what to do next. What's more, for each exercise, I used to have to remember what weight and repetitions I was doing.

What I did, was I began taking a small notepad with me. Before I went, I would have the exercises, weights and repetitions all written down. All in the order I was going to perform them.

When I finished each exercise, I would write down the weight I used and the repetitions. This meant that I would know where I was at next time.

What were the results?

Instead of spending up to two hours in the gym, I was in and out in forty to forty-five minutes. As a bonus, I actually started to get better results. I guess this was due to training more intensely.

I found it a lot easier having a plan. I didn't need to spend time thinking any more. I could just get stuck in and follow my plan.

Now you may be saying that you know about planning. You may already do that. If you do, that's great. However, there are lots of people who don't. Even if they do plan, they often don't plan enough.

The proof is that during the task, despite having a plan, they are still thinking and making decisions. You need to put everything down in your plan. Leave nothing out. Plan beforehand so no thinking is required.

Having everything planned out, works for anything.

Plans are always behind efficiency and are designed for the best results. Think of business plans. How about the NASA space program? Every time they send up the space shuttle, do you think they do it without planning? Of course not. The idea is ludicrous.

So, take out the thinking during the task. Get a plan.

How to plan each task

Sit down in advance and write down what it is you wish to accomplish. This is your goal, if you like.

Next up, is decide what things need to be completed before the end result can be achieved.

When you have this list, try to think about the way you are going to complete each part. (You will learn later a very effective way of doing this.)

When you've done these things, put everything in order. Organise them in steps. In other words, what you do first, second, third, and so on.

This is pretty basic stuff. Here is an example...

Imagine your task is to organise a meeting for your boss.

Write down what people you will need to contact. Hotels, travel agents, taxi firms, venues, etc. Write down all the things you need to arrange.

Next write down what you need to do in order. What comes first, second, and so on. Plan it all out.

When you do all this first, you will be able to sit down and just follow your plan. Everything will work just like clockwork. No thinking time needed.

Don't use a time schedule or calender

Having a schedule can actually be detrimental. You will be learning, later on, a way of prioritising your tasks for the day. However, you would do better by not putting it on a calender or daily planner. The type of planner where you put a time and/or day to do something.

Why?

I bet you will have experienced this before. You start your day and go to your first task. Half way through, something comes up. Something you can't ignore. You must attend to this new matter and put aside what you are doing.

An hour or so later, you decide to go back and finish your original task. But now you notice your next planned task is only an hour away. You try to rush through to complete it in time. What happens is that you probably make mistakes or don't do as good a job as you intended. Or, more than likely, you don't complete the task.

You decide to try fitting it into your planner for another time. However, the next time, other things mess up your plan again. Before you know it, you have several unfinished tasks. You have results that aren't as good as intended. I think you'll agree, not a great result.

What is the solution?

The solution is to just prioritise your tasks but don't put a time or date on it. Simply do one task at a time. See it through from start to finish. If this is not possible, then you may want to delegate the task to someone else.

You will learn later how to prioritise tasks for the best results. When you do this, you will be able to complete one task at a time. If things come up, you can go back to finish your task later. You won't have another scheduled task coming up to interrupt you. When you complete the task, then you can move unto the next.

The message is clear. Don't work to a time schedule. Otherwise things can easily be messed up. Instead, using the prioritisation method, you'll learn later, simply work through one task at a time. You'll be able to do this, because you will have already put everything in order of importance. Work through your list one by one. Finish one before moving to the next.

Of course, the exception to scheduling a time, is for meetings and appointments. The reason is that it synchronises with other people involved. For everything else, just work through your list.

Summary

Reduce the time of all your tasks by removing the thinking part. Formulate a plan. Don't leave anything out. Do all your thinking during planning and not during.

Don't use your calender or set times for tasks. Things often go wrong. Do one task at a time from start to finish before moving unto the next. You won't need to worry about a schedule this way.

Chapter 9: How To Prioritize Your Day-

The 8 Strategies

Time is a very valuable and limited commodity. We have 24 hours in a day and how someone utilizes those few hours is dependent on skills learnt via good planning, evaluation, self-examination and self-control. Good time management often leads to better productivity, less stress, more energy to accomplish things and positive relations. Here are some time management tools:

1.Know you priorities

Effective time management needs you to make a clear difference and contrast between what is more urgent and crucial.

You can create a to-do' list to help you in setting priorities. The to-do list may at times get out of hand if you keep many lists at the same time.

Be careful on the number of lists you make, and rank the things on the list according to how urgent they are. It is for you to decide whether you need daily, weekly or monthly lists. In addition to to-do lists, you can have appointment books. This is because to-do lists may at times become too long to the point that they are unworkable.

2. Avoid procrastination

People usually put off completing a task, maybe because it is too difficult or unpleasant. If you are a procrastinator:

- Exercise dividing the task into smaller parts that need less commitment time.
- If you are finding it challenging to start, do some preparations like gathering materials or sorting your notes.
- Do the difficult stuff first.
- Give yourself consistent breaks so as to rejuvenate yourself.
- Get rid of distractions like answering phone calls and emails, Facebook, Twitter and other social media unless you need them for your work.
- Avoid being a perfectionist because it will waste you a lot of time.
- You can motivate yourself by rewarding yourself every time you finish a task.

3. Do not multi-task

Brain studies show that multi-tasking does not help one to save time so by multi-tasking, you actually waste more time. When shifting from one task to the other, you lose valuable time, and the overall productivity is seriously impaired. A study exposed that the brain needs a minimum of 15 minutes to switch from one activity to another.

Continuous multitasking results in difficulty in concentration and focus.Here are more reasons to avoid multi-tasking:

- It slows you down.
- You end up making more mistakes.
- You get stressed out.
- You end up missing out on life.
- Your memory suffers.
- It may hurt your relationships with other people.
- It may lead to overeating.
- Multitasking ruins your creativity.
- It can be dangerous to multi-task depending on the activity(operating heavy machinery,driving,etc).

4. Delegate your duties to other people(Outsourcing)

Assigning some of your tasks to another person allows you create extra time to tackle jobs that need your expertise. The delegation process starts by recognizing the tasks that other people can carry out and choosing the best person for the job.

Delegation is important for:

- *Efficiency*: delegation enhances efficiency by allowing transfer of jobs to individuals whose skillset is a better match for the task.

- *Development*: being a team leader, you have crucial skills and capabilities that you can pass down to your teammates. Delegation is a good method of encouraging your teammates to develop their abilities and for you to grow your teaching and mentoring abilities.

5. Set time to rest and reenergize

Numerous studies show that the most productive individuals are those that allocate time to rest, exercise and rejuvenate. Beginning earlier or skipping meals might make you more productive sometimes, but if you constantly do this you'll end up stressed and worn-out. Don't fear taking lunch or coffee breaks as in the long run, you will achieve more than the ones who don't take breaks.

While on holiday, switch off work entirely. Don't get tempted to call the office or open your emails. It is important to judge people on what they accomplish, not on how much time they put in, as stress, depression and anxiety are common problems in the society.

6. Finalize your day

Have a personal meeting with yourself each day. Take an hour before leaving the office so as to take a look at what you have accomplished in the day. You might also want to have a diary for the performance judgment. Look at the schedule you have for the next couple of days to know the meetings and deadlines you have.

Prioritize your to-do list again so that you can hit the ground sprinting the following day, and note down all the emerging tasks that has appeared throughout the day that should be done. When you become an expert at doing this, you will close your day having less anxiety about the coming day, and you will end up being more available for your relatives and friends.

7. Get rid of distractions

Continuous distractions disrupt your concentration and may even lower your IQ when doing crucial tasks. If you want to deliver efficient work, turn off all the possible interruptions, such as emails, phone calls, Facebook, twitter and other social media, and devote your time to crucial activities. Choose the appointments that require a reminder, and the time difference between an alert and the meeting.

Check on your emails a limited number of times in the day unless it is absolutely necessary. It may be difficult for many, but you will be surprised at how much more you can accomplish when you are not consistently viewing and replying to emails the whole day.

8. Be insistent on having meeting agendas

A shoddily planned meeting is one of the biggest time wasters. If a meeting you're supposed to attend lacks an agenda, you should decline to attend. If an agenda is not in place, how can you foretell if you are required for the entire meeting or if you're even required at all?

Agendas are important because:

- They set the correct tone since the participants are aware that there is a legitimate commercial purpose for the meeting.
- They identify the discussion topics.
- They keep the people focused.
- They eliminate occurrence of excuses.

At the end of each day, we all want to be proud of how we have utilized our time. A wasted day leads to anxiety, stress and depression at time. Planning your day strategically can help improve your productivity and better your health.

Chapter 10: Commit To Change

Procrastination is the cancer of modern times. It is what hinders you from growing, achieving your goals, and becoming successful.The biggest problem **people have a hard time starting an important task** is that people bite off too much. Make your quota low so you can "succeed" each day. One hugely successful ghost writer (50+ books, including NYT bestsellers) told me his secret to success: just two crappy pages per day. That's all he had to write to "win" for the day, and of course, he often wrote more.

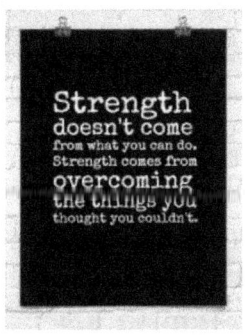

The First Step Is Awareness

If resistance has kicked your butt for a long time, but you don't know how to even start to change it, first thing first, you need to define your fears, the worst-case scenario if you take action, and accept it, embrace it.

Next, think about the cost/damage of continuing to postpone action: what will it look like in 7 days, 30 days, and 365 days? How will it affect you financially, emotionally and psychologically? Recognize that putting off decisions is making a decision: to push yourself to failure.

I assume you had enough of postpone and wanted so badly to change. That's why you are reading this book. You want to be a more productive and complete the damn thing that you started but drag for century, and guess what? You couldn't be anywhere more suitable than here. I just need one thing from you. Only one thing.

Secret Sauce that Guarantee Success

So let's be straight forward. You can have all the solutions, techniques, secret way found in this book to beat procrastinate but nothing would ever happen until you commit and trust the system. Now read out loud with me. Commit and trust the system, commit and trust the system, commit and trust the system. No one will ever succeed in anything/ change anything/ achieve anything without really commit to it.

The powerful solutions presented in this book are straightforward and easy to follow. To get started, you do not have to adopt everything. Start with just one habit and focus on building that. Before you know it, you already have kicked procrastination out of your life.

So, are you ready for a change? If you are, then allow us to lead you through the path for a successful and productive life!

Chapter 11: Making Meditation A Part Of

Your Daily Life

"I don't have the time to meditate!" This is the most common thing I hear while I am sharing my experiences about meditation with people I know. I am sure you too would be thinking of saying the same thing. It's perfectly normal. I too had the same reaction before starting off. You are so caught up with the routine that you tend to just go with the flow without thinking. You seem to be so busy with work, kids, laundry, groceries and cooking that you have no time for anything.

The answer to this is simple – Start Meditating Today! It cannot get more real than this. If you are the kind who just cannot find the time to meditate, my message for you Is – Make time for Meditation! You have to make meditation a priority in your life.

When I had my first kid, I used to find it really tough to stick to the meditation schedule that I set for myself. I was more of a nocturnal animal who had to attend to the needs of my newborn, leaving me completely drained out by morning. Meditation seemed far-fetched because I was far from being patient. As days passed I started getting anxious as I wasn't really able to connect with myself midst all the chaos. Slowly and steadily, I started figuring out ways to incorporate meditation into my daily routine and now I can share with you simple steps that worked for me.

Like every human being, I chose the path of least resistance and came up with these easy steps that will enable you to include meditation in your life. I challenge you that with these steps, you can meditate anytime and anywhere – even when you partake in your routine chores. Gone are the days when you needed a meditation pillow and a few minutes in the morning to meditate. These tips will break that myth for you. Meditation can transcend in any facet of your life if you do it effectively and consistently. The following steps will take a lot of determination and dedication at your end.

Make a Meditation Schedule and Stick with it: Decide on a time during the day when you find it comfortable to meditate and stick to it, come what may. Look at meditation like one of the 'must-dos' of the day. The biggest obstacle to this is you yourself. You will keep coming up with novel excuses to procrastinate your meditative sessions. Don't give in to this temptation. Make it a habit. When you do that you will get accustomed to it and the comfort level will keep going up. Once you start, you will feel uneasy if you do not meditate. This happens with me often. Since meditation is a habit for me, I feel extremely out of place if I miss it even once. It's like brushing your teeth. Don't you feel filthy if you do not start your day by brushing or bathing?

My suggestion: No matter what time you are up in the morning, meditate for 15 minutes. Start your day with meditation. Once you start, dedicate that time for it every single day. In case you have some unavoidable task to perform, you can always reschedule your session.

Be Creative: Meditation is primarily concentrating on your thoughts while not letting your mind wander away. Sometimes think differently. Think out-of-the-box as to how you can incorporate meditation in everything you do.

Meditate while brushing your teeth: Focus on what you are doing. Look at yourself in the mirror with a gentle smile and remind yourself of how you want to take care of every part of your body. Don't rush through brushing and rinsing. Instead, do it slowly and gently while contemplating on what you are doing.

Meditate while You Drive: I definitely don't mean that you should close your eyes or not pay attention to the traffic on the road. Instead, be calm and aware of all the things around you. Keep your mobile on a silent mode and drive in complete silence. Don't let other drivers and the excessive traffic on the road bother you. Look around with a calm mind and be aware of all that's happening without reacting.

Meditate at Work: Be mindful of your workplace. Keep interacting with colleagues and responding to emails in a patient and calm manner. Practice responding to a situation rather than reacting. When you do this, your colleagues and mail recipients will also be able to experience your state of mind. Contemplate on your thoughts, words and action while at work.

Meditate while Exercising: Allow meditation to be a part of your life while you exercise. So instead of watching a movie while exercising, concentrate on each and every muscle you are working out on. Pay attention to each move you make and how it is playing a role in improving the blood circulation in your body. Concentrate on how the workout is nourishing every cell in your body.

Meditate while Cooking: Cooking can be very therapeutic in itself. When my mother makes something with a lot of positive emotions and love, I can feel it. So while you are cooking, let go of any anxieties and fears. Think of all the nourishment you are about to provide to your loved ones through this food. Pay close attention to every ingredient you are adding. Shun every negative emotion and think of passing on your love and care to your family through this meal.

Keep a Dedicated Place for Meditation: A quiet and peaceful place is essential for a successful meditative session. Dedicate an area in your house or in a park nearby to meditate. Ensure you are not distracted by anything in the place you choose. Also, check for enough space around you so that you can seat yourself comfortably. If you are dedicating a room in your house, make sure it is devoid of distractions like the television, radio or a music system.

Simply Breathe: There are thousands of books talking about '**asanas**' and breathing techniques to attain a meditative state. Don't get too technical. Just keep it simple and do what works for you. Just start off with some mindful breathing. This means you need to focus on your breathing. This has 3 distinct benefits:

☐ It calms you down instantly and helps you concentrate on your current state.

☐ It is very basic and easy. Everyone who wants to live breathes! All I am suggesting is to pay close attention to your breathing. You will not have to wait for long to get into a meditative state by doing this simple activity.

☐ You can breathe anywhere and anytime.

Practice Mindfulness in Your Regular Life too: Don't just wait for a meditative session to practice mindfulness. When you practice it in everything you do, you become a changed person. You are more calm and patient. You are at peace with yourself and find solutions to problems rather than complaining about them. Make it a daily habit and see how it changes your personality. The more you are exposed to a particular thing the more you start accepting it as a part of you. It becomes your way of life. Moreover, you will fascinate others around you with your positive aura. They will want to know the secret behind your happy and calm mind.

Resolve to Meditate Twice a day: Just like you do in the morning, practice meditation before you go to bed. The length of time you practice it for is completely based on your comfort level. If you find it tough to sit for 20 minutes at a stretch, split it into 2 different slots of 10 minutes each.

I am sure that if you incorporate these steps in your life, you will be able to incorporate meditation into your life effortlessly.

Chapter 12: Which One Of These Five

Types Of Procrastinator Are You?

Before we start to help you dealing with the procrastination habit, it is important for you to identify which type of procrastinator you are. Of course, it is highly possible that you can relate with several or all of these types more or less. With this knowledge, you can detect more easily which solutions you can find in the last chapter of this book would be the most relevant for you.
The Perfectionist
This type of procrastinator is the most common one. If you are a perfectionist you tend to set standards to yourself that are too high to accomplish. Perfectionists become overwhelmed of the tasks ahead. In contrast to other procrastinators, they tend to have an easier time with starting to work on tasks, however they usually have a hard time to finish them. Due to the fact, that they are afraid that they

cannot do something perfectly and meet their unrealistic expectations, nothing gets done at all in the worst case.

The Avoider

People who tend to avoid tasks usually think that their duties at hand are too dreadful, unnecessary or risky. Avoiders oftentimes focus on the opinions of other people and run away from their fear of failure or even success.

The Hedonist

Hedonists are people who believe that they thrive and do their best work when they are under pressure. They procrastinate, since they love the adrenaline kick and feel that accomplishing tasks last minute makes the process less boring. However, spending so little time on projects hinders them to reach their full potential most of the time.

The Dreamer

Dreamers often find their minds wandering around and getting lost in thought. They have difficulties with distinguishing between elusive dreams and aims that are measurable and specific.

Planning details and carry out a task is a challenge for them.

The Indecisive

Indecisive procrastinators tend to feel overwhelmed by the sheer amount of tasks they have to accomplish, as every one of them feels equally important to them. That is why they cannot decide where to start and as a consequence, they find themselves not having done anything at all.

Chapter 13: Shoring Up The Necessary

Motivation To Succeed

In combatting procrastination, it is necessary that you remain motivated enough to see through your tasks. Otherwise, how else will you muster the energy and inspiration you need to get anything done?

That can be a problem to always have the motivation you need in order to stop procrastinating and succeed. If you are clueless on how to do this, just think of the people you look up to and hold in high esteem. Then ask yourself some of the following questions:

- What is it about them that makes you regard them highly?
- What are the traits and values that you seek to emulate yourself?
- How do you intend to follow in their footsteps?

Having role models is a powerful way to help steer yourself to the path you want to tread. Through the success of others and the insights derived from their experiences, you get to assemble your own idea of what you want to achieve.

If this idea is powerful enough, there's little reason why you should procrastinate because doing so will only keep you from achieving your goals.

Here are other ways to shore up your sense of motivation:

Master goal-setting. Begin by spelling out your goals on a daily basis. Then move on to weekly, monthly, or even yearly goal-setting. The idea is that your actions should be guided by a set of goals that you want to accomplish over time. You don't want to do things without any clear idea of what you want to achieve.

Stay focused. Sport a proactive attitude in doing away with any form of unhealthy distraction as much as possible. The reason most people procrastinate is because they can't keep their focus on what they are doing.

Learn from the past. Dwell on best practices or those things that allowed you to succeed in the past. At the same time, pay attention to your mistakes and make sure you don't repeat them.

Learn to relax. A sure-fire formula for getting burned out is if you don't take a much-needed breather when you should. Recharge and reinvigorate yourself every now and then. You need to be at your best all the time, so take measures to ensure you get the rest you deserve.

Do not be complacent. Always strive for bigger goals without compromising your ability to remain reasonable and realistic. The more you get comfortable to a certain routine or set-up, the greater the chance that you procrastinate. Challenge yourself always.

Find people or resources to help you. Continue to seek opportunities for growth either by enrolling at school, learning a new skill, and taking part in professional trainings, skills enhancement classes and mentoring programs.

Foster greater positivity in your life. It helps to position yourself in the company of positive people or those who are motivated enough to succeed. Be challenged by healthy competition. Lend support and share insights with each other.

Take time to learn and practice what you've learned. The more you learn the more capable you will feel and this will build your self-confidence so the more challenging tasks don't seem so challenging anymore. As with all things, you should allow these insights to take root in your life.

These are all great tools you can start to apply immediately. There is still more work to be done though. The next chapter discusses the debilitating effects of procrastination in both your personal and professional life.

Chapter 14: Dropping The Distractions

Procrastinators always have a reason why they have not done something. They are very good at making excuses and much of the time the excuses are not valid ones. The fact that you spent two hours catching up with what your Facebook friends are up to, or stalking your neighbor on LinkedIn isn't anyone's fault but yours. These are all distractions that stop you from achieving. You need to learn something very valuable about distractions. When you have goals, switch off the distractions. The Facebook page will look the same later when you have finished your work. Switch off your mobile phone. Stop looking for alerts. Life existed before all of these distractions happened and they really do hold you back and make you less productive than you could be. If you intend doing something at home, turn off your phone, put a message on your answerphone to tell people when they can get you and forget about the world outside your home. When you are at work, switch off anything that involves social media except anything that is really work related. However, when you have things to do that don't involve social media, switch it off. It's a real time waster and your life is being lived virtually rather than in reality.

Using a timer

You may not be aware of it, but it's an art that was developed a while back that helps you to become more productive. If you split your work day into sections you help yourself to achieve more and I will tell you how to do it. When you have a job you hate, but you know needs doing, set aside time to do it. Then turn on the timer. While the timer is ticking you work solidly for a period of 45 minutes. Then you can get up from your work and walk around, taking a break and getting yourself a cup of coffee or a glass of water. Don't get into looking at your social networks. You only have a ten minute break. Then go back to your desk and reset the timer for 45 minutes and concentrate during this time totally on the job that you have to do. After you have done this several times, you can make the next break a bit longer, for example for your lunch break. Get up from your desk, go out into the sunshine and breathe. Enjoy the space that you have placed between work and private life.

The best time to do this is always going to be first thing in the morning and you may need to forewarn colleagues that you have something that needs your concentration so that they don't bother you during that time. Your boss may even have a quiet room where you can work to reach those deadlines. First thing in the morning, your brain is at its most active so you can achieve more and if you use the timer, you are restricting yourself in a way that helps you to achieve all that you have to do within the time you have given yourself.

Measure what you do

We all have jobs that are boring and repetitive. For example, you may find yourself writing very similar emails all day long to clients who ask the same questions. While you have no distractions, make out templates that you can use to help you to get through the emails in your inbox. Make sure that you have your signature already in the email and use these templates to make short work of the emails that you need to answer. If you have filing to do, give yourself a time limit and measure what you do. Perhaps today you filed 40 papers. Tomorrow you can aim at 60. You don't need to tell anyone you are doing this. It's for your own satisfaction rather than for anyone else. What you are doing by measuring your work is making yourself quicker at what you do and thus cutting down the number of hours that you need to spend on mundane tasks.

All of these tasks are better when there are no distractions. Contrary to popular belief, your brain was not made to multi-task and you can never give your best attention to something if your mind is elsewhere, trying to multi task. You can have fun when the work is done, but don't use the fun as your excuse not to have the time to perform the duties that you are asked to do. They are not valid excuses.

They are what lazy people use as excuses and there is a big difference.

Chapter 15: Uncover Your Habits And

Patterns

Habit formation is closely linked to self-discipline. When you form good habits and stick to them, you will be able to improve your productivity as you work towards your goals. On the other hand, it is possible to form habits and patterns that make you become undisciplined. As such, you may find yourself procrastinating and being unproductive not because you don't know what to do but simply because you've allowed negative habits to corrode your discipline.

It has been said before that human beings are creatures of habit. This in itself is not a bad thing. However, you need to make it work for you. You need to get rid of bad habits and embrace habits that will actually enable you to achieve your goals.

It is important to note that both bad and good habits are formed in the same way. Essentially, three components make up a habit. These are:

The Trigger or Cue

A habit starts with a cue or trigger. This trigger signals the unfolding of the habit. For example, if you are used to eating your lunch at noon, you will find yourself thinking of food as soon as the clock nears noontime. In this case, the time becomes the trigger. You want to eat just because it is lunchtime, not because you are hungry. If you are too busy to notice the time, you may not think of food until much later.

The Routine

Here is the thing. Habits are formed due to repetition. When you routinely do something, it becomes easier to do it to the point that you do not give much thought to it after awhile. You just do it.

A habit starts with a cue and is followed by a series of behavior. Over time, it becomes a pattern of behavior and you learn to do it almost automatically. For example, many people remove their shoes, loosen their clothes, throw their keys on the table and their bag on a nearby surface and go in search of something to eat or reach for the remote, whenever they arrive home from work or school. That is their routine. It starts right after they see that door to their home and it signals that they are ready to 'unwind' and leave the stresses of work behind.

Such routines become second nature simply because they have been repeated over and over. You need not think too much, about what you're doing, and at times, it takes someone else to point out that you've 'left your things on the floor for you to be aware of what you've done.

The Reward

If you do something and it brings you pleasant results, you will want to do it again. This is because it is gratifying. You feel like you have received a reward because you have engaged in the activity.

A reward is anything that brings you gratification. It can be a feeling of satisfaction, a pat on the back from someone or even monetary gain. When you receive a reward, your brain learns to associate that activity with pleasant feelings.

For example, watching funny videos brings about feelings of happiness. You may find yourself watching such videos instead of doing your work. The videos bring instant gratification and thus watching them proves more desirable.

Always understand that every habit has a cue, a routine and a reward. Of the three components, the cue and the reward are what you need to focus on. This is because the cue signals the start of the habit or behavior. If you know what triggers the habit or when it starts, you will be able to stop it in its tracks before it fully forms or, you'll find the motivation to keep at it if it is a habit you want to fully embrace.

But what about the reward?

What happens after you have engaged in an activity will determine if you will go on with it or not. For example, a kid who receives attention after throwing a tantrum is likely to throw more tantrums in future because it gets him what he needs in terms of attention. In this case, he continues the bad behavior because he is rewarded for it.

But there is something else you need to know about rewards. Habits that bring instant rewards or gratification are more desirable than habits that bring about long term results. For example, you may find yourself watching funny videos rather than finishing a project. This is because the former activity brings about instant gratification while you will have to wait awhile to see the results brought about by the latter activity. This is why it is important to examine your habits.

What are your habits or pattern of behavior? What triggers them? What reward do you get when you do? If you learn the answer to these questions, you will be a step closer to reigning in your actions. You will be fully aware of the situations that lead you to become undisciplined and thus, you will be able to take a step back and make better decisions.

However, there's something else you need to note.

Habits need not be 'bad' for them to be disruptive. You can easily find yourself engaging in various activities throughout the day without actually doing what you were meant to do. This is known as procrastination.

Procrastination is a habit. It is harmful in that it disguises itself as productivity. It makes you think that you are accomplishing a lot only to find out that you were 'busy doing nothing'. That is, at the end of the day, you have not accomplished what you were meant to accomplish.

If you allow procrastination and other bad habits to encroach on your life, you will find it difficult to accomplish your goals. On the other hand, if you take control of your life and increase your mental toughness, you will be able to beat procrastination and achieve your goals. One effective way to re-establish control is by setting SMART goals. Let's see how you can do that.

Chapter 16: Naming It And Taming It.

As I related in the introduction, it took losing a job I loved to teach me the lesson I needed to learn. When you lose something precious to you, if you're not reflecting on why you lost it, then you're not benefiting from the experience.

A negative experience can be transformed by the act of looking inside yourself for the answers, instead of blaming those around you, a "heartless system", a "mean boss", or a "hostile world".

Those are excuses. You're the source of the problem and admitting that to yourself is your first step toward breaking the bad habits and overcoming the laziness holding you back in life.

Getting out of your own way is a process that begins with having the courage to name yourself as the roadblock.

If you can do that, you can do anything.

Step 1: Naming the problem.

You're going to stand in front of the nearest mirror and say the following to yourself: "I need to change to succeed."

What's important for you to understand at this early stage of the game is that everyone needs to change to succeed. People who tread water in life tend to have habits which get in the way of their path to a successful life.

You need to change, just as everyone else does. You have bad habits. You're a little lazy. Those are human traits, so don't allow yourself to descend into negative thinking that causes you to cast yourself as a misfit, or worse. Use the experience of naming yourself as the problem as a type of rebirth.

You are intentionally rebirthing yourself as a productive presence in the world.

It sounds counter-intuitive, but it's not. Self-transformation is work. It's hard work. The hardest part is getting started. If you're at that point and can admit that you're the source of the problem, then you're already doing more than most are willing to do.

Being honest with yourself about your shortcomings isn't easy. That's why far too many people avoid doing it. By standing in front of the mirror and telling yourself the straight up truth, you're already a hero. You're being reborn in the image of a better version of you.

Step 2: Confronting your habits

Procrastination happens when you let your bad habits get the better of you. You're at work and it's 11:30 am. Instead of tying up some loose ends before you head out to lunch, you venture onto your Facebook page. There, you see a discussion in progress about someone you know. You jump into the comments section and offer your opinion, unable to resist the siren call of online gossip.

You are procrastinating. You have taken time that doesn't belong to you (because you're on the clock, at work) and squandered it on a fleeting, largely useless weakness for personal scuttlebutt that not only doesn't serve you, but can get you in trouble with your superiors – and that person you're talking about.

Confronting habits like this is a matter of making rules for yourself (which we'll talk about more later in this book). Discipline is a choice we make. It's self-regulation. By regulating your bad habits, you're carving out needed time to get things done. That's what you're getting paid for.

Procrastination happens when you meander aimlessly from co-worker desk to co-worker desk and become embroiled in chitter chatter. You all have things to do, but you'd rather be passing the time of day and avoiding those things. It's easy to rationalize time-wasting behaviors like "visiting" at work. You're cementing co-worker relationships, you're team-building. But whatever you want to call it, it's wasting time.

Have brief conversations, and then move on. Make a rule for yourself around visiting at work. Take note of those who seem to be engaged in non-work-related conversations every day, with a variety of people, then resolve to find ways to avoid engaging them. You have better things to do and you're being paid to do them.

Make a list of procrastination behaviors you engage in that are undermining your effectiveness at work. Next to each behavior, write down your plan for breaking the habit. Having a plan in black and white is a promise to yourself you'll be less inclined to break.

This is the foundational document of your professional rebirth, so keep it with you and refer to it when you feel yourself backsliding down the procrastination rabbit hole.

Step 3: Defining your goals.

You're reading this because you know that procrastination has gotten in the way of your goals. Your bad habits and tendency to be lazy has hit you right in your career.

As I've already revealed, that's exactly what happened to me. My foot-dragging and lolly-gagging had an almost disastrous effect on my career. But I was brave enough to name the problem, confront my bad habits and in so doing, was able to define my goals.

What I wanted was what a lot of people want — a clear path to successful living. I wanted to do more than just exist. I wanted to thrive doing work that was fulfilling and engaging. But to get there, I had to change.

Once I'd defined my goals, I discovered that it was much easier to tame habits that were holding me back. I realized that what I did every day was a step on the path toward my goals. And that's an important point.

What you do every day is a step on the path toward your goals. It's not just showing up and doing the minimum required to keep your job. It's about completing every task as though it mattered and the truth is that every task does matter, regardless of how thankless you may think it is.

When you wake up to the reality that the "daily grind" is part of a trajectory you're on that should be moving you toward what you really want, work takes on a whole new significance. You're doing more than earning a paycheck. Even if you're working for somebody else, you're working for yourself. What you do today impacts what you'll be doing tomorrow, for better or worse.

I changed the way I thought about work and came to the realization that each day was part of a whole and ripe with the potential to achieve.

Defining your goals in life is a kick in the pants you can't afford not to take. That kick in the pants is going to getting you moving in the direction you want to go, because it's easier to get somewhere when you have a clear roadmap.

You are your own GPS. You decide which direction you're going to go in. That major decision consists of an ongoing series of micro-decisions which are propelling you to a conclusion. It's never too late to change your life's trajectory, but it's you who decides. Not a "mean boss". Not a "hostile world". Not an "unfair review". It's you.

Take a moment now to think about what you really want to achieve. Are you working toward something, or are you just showing up and warming a chair so you can take home a paycheck? Do you need to step up at work, or do you need to step into another job?

Maybe you want to start your own business, or become an independent contractor. Great ideas, but guess what? Entrepreneurs and contractors don't have anyone looking over their shoulders to ensure they get things done. They do it as a way of life. It's who they are and it's who you can be, if your goal is to join their ranks.

While you're breaking your bad habits, motivational impetus can be found in looking outside your current situation and finding the route by which you're going to get to where you want to go. The more you know about the direction you're going in, the more likely it is you're going to re-calibrate yourself to be ready to get to your destination.

And there's great power in that. When you define your goals, you face each day with a destination in mind. Instead of sitting in the back seat and letting others drive, you're at the wheel – in control.

In the next chapter, we're going to look at some practical ways you can replace bad habits with good ones and laziness with action. Now that you have the basic framework for ending procrastination, we're going to flesh out some of the details.

Chapter 17: Motivate Yourself

One of the more difficult things to do regarding increased productivity is finding ways to keep yourself motivated. But while this is difficult, it is absolutely necessary. Motivation or a lack thereof is the real reason people procrastinate on their duties. Finding a way to combat this is crucial.

Firstly, it is our human nature to use fear as a motivating tool. This is not always the most psychologically beneficial route to take. It is emotionally stressful to think of the worst possible scenario as a means of motivating ourselves to work. If you are always thinking about losing your job, or failing that test, or not getting into the college you want, your brain becomes preoccupied with negativity. Do not underestimate the damaging toll that pervasive negative thoughts have on your brain. You can easily begin thinking that nothing good can ever happen and that you are constantly living on the edge between success and failure. The best way to combat this is to simply calm down and motivate yourself with positivity. Rather than thinking about the awful things that will happen if you fail to complete that project at work, think about the great things that can happen if you do a good job. In this way, you will be focused on positivity and not negativity. We all want to succeed. Why not motivate ourselves with the reward of success rather the fear of failure?

This has a second advantage regarding the quality of our work. If we are motivated not to fail, that will often motivate us only to work hard enough to stick around. In other words, if what we fear is losing our jobs, we may turn in a project on time, but it may be weak and sloppy. Likewise, if our goal is to remain in school, we will complete our homework but it might be wrong or lazily done. Consider the alternative. If our goal is to get a promotion or to get on the honor roll, we will hold our own work to a higher standard. You do not get ahead in life by doing mediocre work. We aren't aiming to do just enough to get by; we are aiming to be more productive and to succeed.

Along the same lines, you might find motivation in other people's success stories. We are obviously all very busy and adding an additional task oftentimes seems ridiculous in the face of so much to do. That said, it can be very beneficial to read up on the success of other people and the processes they used to become successful. Nobody gets there overnight.

If you understand the mentality of people who have accomplished a lot you can set yourself on a similar course. Again, this is motivation by positivity. Do not think of the worst-case scenario; think of the best case scenario.

You would also do well to visualize your goals each day. This sounds silly but thinking about your own productivity and the success you hope to have keeps you on track. When I was in graduate school, I would think constantly about the vision of receiving my Master's Degree. Nobody in my family had ever gone to graduate school before and I knew my family was going to be very proud. I visualized my grandmother and the pride on her face during my graduation. These small things kept me working throughout the process. Visualizing the nice things at the end of the tunnel is also helpful.

Lastly, be mindful not to make mountains out of molehills. It is easy to get discouraged throughout the process. Discouragement leads to a high rate of quitting. And this is unacceptable. Remember that nobody goes through life without some bumps in the road. Just because the process got hard does not mean that you should quit. Keep in mind all of the successful people that had many failures throughout their lives. Michael Jordan was cut from his high school basketball team. Oprah Winfrey was demoted from her news anchor job because she wasn't "fit for television." Walt Disney was fired from his newspaper job for lacking "imagination and creativity." Failures can actually be a good thing. Use them as motivational rocket fuel and keep going.

Chapter 18: Benefits When You Stop

Procrastinating

When you stop procrastinating, you will notice the vast benefits that follow. In this chapter, we will discuss the 4 main benefits that you may see after you start to overcome procrastination.

For Your Studies

When it comes to studying, many people have distractions and choose to watch a movie, telephone their friend or go outside to avoid spending the afternoon studying. Sometimes we can afford an afternoon off; but when you actually stop procrastinating, you are more likely to improve your academic performance and have more control over your life. Procrastinating students intend to carry out the required task, but their brain instead decides to replace that with something easy and fun. Those who suffer from this usually have motivational problems, short attention spans, and are easily distracted; they do not know how to make the most of their capacity for paying attention.

If this sounds like you, create specific goals and ask someone for help to monitor you. Discipline yourself to face the tasks that you do not want to do, divide the tasks into small parts, and work to short deadlines. You will get better results, and little by little you will begin to change the bad habits into positive ones, allowing you to be one step closer to success.

For Your Career

If you are a manager or leader, you usually instruct people to perform specific tasks and set deadlines for them. If the assigned people do not fulfill their obligations, you can hold them responsible and potentially use disciplinary measures. When you manage the schedule effectively, employees dedicate more of their working hours to important tasks, which can increase productivity and income for the company. When you handle the costs, you can also avoid unforeseen circumstances like a fraud.

If you are an employee and try to stop procrastinating, you will be much more productive; you will finish the work you did before in much less time and at a higher standard.

The feeling of completing an assigned task can be more satisfying than all the congratulations of the world; it is something incomparable, as it has the advantage that you can keep doing that good work through conscientious preparation.

Decreasing Your Stress Levels

Once you stop procrastinating, you will have the more free time or at least you can finish your projects without rushing. When you handle your money well, you can worry less about how you're going to pay your expenses. Similarly, overcoming procrastination has the potential to reduce your stress level.

You will have more control over your life because you will know what you should do and when you will have extra time for yourself. You will be able to devote yourself to the things you like and not just the things you have to do.

This control translates to having less stress because when you have control over your time and your life, you immediately feel much calmer and relaxed.

Productivity in Your Life

Consider the example of someone who procrastinates losing weight. In many cases, the solution is to keep a stringent diet so as to lose weight quickly. For a few months, the procrastinator can lose a lot of weight and feel motivated. However, a weight-loss diet cannot be maintained for too long because it isn't always healthy and requires discipline.

Personal productivity is the same. Our task lists are overloaded with bad habits: procrastinating at work and not resting properly in our personal time. We are only interested in productivity techniques when we are overwhelmed. But it is important to realize that if we are always aware of the dangers of procrastination, we are less likely to fall back into the same habits; we need to have discipline.

Therefore, we shouldn't wait until we have too many tasks. Personal productivity is a way of understanding life and helps us avoid taking on more than we can handle

Chapter 19: Why You Need A Morning

Routine

I was never a morning person; in fact, I always thought I could never be one. However, because I am a driven person and my business demanded that I wake up early and prepare for the day ahead, I decided to become a morning person. As I started researching the subject, I discovered how beneficial it was to have a morning routine; this discovery motivated me to develop one.

If like me, you think you cannot have an effective morning routine that prepares you for success throughout the day, you are wrong and like me, the only thing you need to get started is some motivation.

In this chapter, we will discuss various reasons why you need a morning routine and the beneficial effects a morning routine has on your life. Before we look at these benefits, let us start by discussing what a morning routine is.

The Psychology Behind A Morning Routine

Your morning routine is the set of rituals you perform to have a happy, energetic, and productive start to your day. Your morning routine sets the tone for the rest of the day.

For instance, if you wake up 10 minutes before you are due to start working or supposed to be at work, you will have no time and will have to rush through your morning. However, if you develop a morning routine that gives you even a half-hour of 'me' time, your day will start on the right footing.

Because we live in a fast-paced world, we barely get time to spend with ourselves. A morning routine gives you the chance to indulge in self-love especially when you make a morning routine a ritual you cycle through every day.

For instance, if before you leave for work, you give yourself an hour, you can fill that time with a morning ritual such as spending time with your family, eating a healthy breakfast, or meditation.

Morning routines vary from person to person because what works for one person may not work for another. This is the best thing about having a morning routine: you focus only on yourself.

One thing all successful people have in common is a morning routine. Barrack Obama, Oprah Winfrey, and Tony Robbins have repeatedly emphasized the importance of a morning routine.

Why You Need A Morning Routine

Now that we have established what a morning routine is, let us look at the benefits you stand to derive from developing a healthy morning routine.

1: Sets a Good Tone for the Day

By engaging in a series of healthy morning rituals, you refresh and energize your mind and body, which sets a positive mood for the entire day. You stay happy and active. When you are happy and active, you are motivated and thus less likely to procrastinate.

For instance, after waking up, I meditate and visualize my goals. I do this every day. This makes me calm, positive, confident, and sets a great tone for the entire day.

This helps me complete my work on time every time.

2: Lets You Practice Self-love

Nowadays, self-love is a rarity because the world is highly demanding, which means we never get any time to spend with ourselves, which then leads to stress, anxiety, and self-hatred.

If you have a morning routine, you spend some 'me' time at the beginning of each day. This makes you happy and allows you to connect with yourself. When you are happy and in synchronicity with your true self, you do things that focus on your wellbeing: things that help you feel good about yourself and your life.

For instance, if you develop a morning routine that involves the ritual of making yourself a healthy, delicious breakfast each morning, you not only get to enjoy some alone time, you also feel important and worthy of being loved and cared for.

3: Makes You Feel Fresh

If you jump right on to the activities planned for the day, you will feel enslaved to your tasks and responsibilities. Your life will be robotic and monotonous. However, by engaging in a few morning rituals that calm and relax you, you feel fresh and active and easily adjust to the chores planned for the day.

Now that you know the benefits of having a morning routine, let us discuss how you can easily develop one.

Chapter 20: Quitting Time

We finished the last chapter with thoughts on the fact that sometimes it is time to let go. When we looked at your to-do list we had a culling of tasks that were unimportant and not urgent and you were told to let them go. The thought of doing so probably caused a little anxiety and you may have said you'll get to them eventually too. Knowing when you've had enough of any task and that it's time to take a break can prevent you wasting time procrastinating instead of working. Multitasking isn't good, but stepping away from one task to focus on a second one may be the reset you need (just don't forget to get back to that first task).

Example:

Felicity is at her job. She has been entering data all day in her computer and while she did take a short break earlier her deadline seems to be coming up fast. She's been pushing all week to get this task done and it seems like it will never end.

While she's sitting at her computer she notices the weather outside. Her thoughts wander to think about whether it's warm enough to cook out, what they could make, whether they have food in the house or if she needs to go to the store, mentally she even makes the shopping list for the drive home. The problem is 20 minutes have now gone and she hasn't entered a thing. Felicity didn't mean to procrastinate so she shakes herself out of it and goes back to entering the data. She finds herself thinking about dinner, the dog, the kids and struggling to put the information in but she keeps on. Finally, she's about done when she realizes that almost everything she's entered for the past 20 minutes is totally wrong. Her unfocused mind entered the same information multiple times into different client boxes so she now has to be back and do it again. While she still wasn't intentionally procrastinating about doing the task her overwork has caused her mind to simply work on autopilot and it's now given her even more work to do. We know when we need a break, we just don't want to take it because it means the task will go on longer. Perhaps it's because you're anticipating that reward at the end or the success of being finished. Being in the middle is where our enthusiasm, focus, and energy lags and it's where we procrastinate most. Taking a break is a precarious thing because you're risking simply not coming back to the task but knowing that the quality of your work is going to suffer means you're not being productive because you risk having to do it again.

Saying No

Sometimes you do need to give up. Eventually, tasks just aren't working or no matter how much you try you simply can't focus on them. The decision to give up can just be a temporary respite unless you really believe that you will never succeed. Examine how you've worked on the task so far and how much effort you've put in. If you haven't really made much of a commitment it may just be time to cut your losses and say enough. Similarly, when you have all the focus in the world it won't help if your to-do list keeps getting longer. When you set your schedule back in chapter three you should have left a certain amount of free time for unexpected tasks and events. This includes someone popping their head in and tossing another folder on your "in" tray or a meeting for a new product etc. If you're starting to feel that this free time is slipping away or you're getting that overwhelming feeling again then it's time to say no.

We have become a culture where "no" is frowned on. By saying no we are admitting we are not invincible and that we have limits. It's a scary thought that has the potential to damage our marketability because people don't like being told no. Learning when to say no is part of preventing procrastination because it allows you to know your limits and stop you reaching that stage of being overwhelmed where nothing gets done.

Accepting your Failures

No matter how hard you try sometimes there are things you won't be good at. It's just a fact, you may never be good at something. While you can continue trying often it's trying to be hard at something you don't understand or that isn't working for you that leads to procrastination. Learning that you have your limits and that you're not the perfect person your procrastination screams for can easily solve most of your problems. By not stressing because you're not perfect and you can't handle everything and you will occasionally fail you're going to feel much lighter. The liberating feel of acceptance that this is out of your control because it's beyond your limit is great. **Tip: if you're the sort of person who really struggles to say no to anything or to speak up practice on your own. Start in front of the mirror and say it firmly to yourself out loud. When you're feeling strongly about something remember that experience and do it again.** The ability to say no has been linked to low self-confidence and a worry that you'll antagonize others. This is a situation where you're going to need to weigh yourself against the task. Which is more important – you or the task? You can even use the Eisenhower diagram to determine this but if you're finding that you are more important than the task because you know it will put you at your limit and cause procrastination then it's time to say no. There are lots of ways to tackle this without being rude and upsetting anyone. Keep your response simple and be sympathetic. You can also buy time by offering to do it at a later date or some other compromise if you truly believe you need to do the task. Compromising and negotiating is rather the way of saying yes without feeling the stress of it. You should only do this if you really want to make time for that thing and not because you feel pressured to do it.

Be honest with yourself during this time, if you need to say no then be honest about it and you can tell the person that you can't, plain and simple.

Procrastination Negotiation

Applying the negotiation principal to yourself can also work when you fail to say no to procrastination. Sometimes you are going to procrastinate. It's a fact that we can't escape unless you're a Type A super driver hyper focused individual, in which case you probably don't need to be reading this book. The key is to simply accept that. Like accepting that you aren't going to be able to do everything accepting that sometimes procrastination happens, shrugging it off and moving on is the best remedy rather than wasting any more time on it.

Think of procrastination like your annoying ex. Rather than letting them continue to bug you simply toss them out the window and forget about them. If you can't because you're still sharing the same space your only choice is to negotiate. Negotiating with your procrastination is essentially what you've been doing with this book. You've created several tasks to draw yourself back, allowed time for procrastination to happen, and get back to what you were doing. Negotiating is a small success. In fact, it would be better if you don't do this, but if you've tried every other method so far and nothing has successfully worked then this might be your only alternative before seeking help for an attention disorder. This is your last chance to conquer your procrastination on a regular basis and if this doesn't work start again at the beginning of this chapter and determine if it's either time to give up or just say no.

Chapter 21: The Science Of Growth

Mindset

A common misconception is that the theory of mindset is just that: a theory. As everyone seeks to self-help titles and topics to assist them in their personal growth, many find themselves lost among all of the different pieces of information floating around. This has resulted in many people not having a strong idea on what growth mindset truly is or about the proof that it genuinely exists. Many don't even believe that this theory has any truth behind it based on a lot of misinformation that is mixed in with the facts.

The fortunate truth is that mindset actually does have very strong scientific roots, and you can use these as evidence that any work you do towards your mindset will hold great power in your ability to have a growth mindset. The rest of this chapter is going to explain the scientific roots of growth mindset, and why this should matter to you.

Theory   **Founder**

The theory of growth mindset was founded over 30 years ago by a lady named Carol Dweck. Alongside her colleagues, they became fascinated in understanding their students' attitudes surrounding the topic of "failure." They developed this interest after seeing two very different reactions to failure in their students: some rebounded and were empowered to do better, and others were devastated no matter how small or large the failure was perceived to be.

Fixed Mindset VS. Growth Mindset

Following many studies involving thousands of students, Carol Dweck coined two terms: fixed mindset and growth mindset. These terms are used to describe each person's underlying beliefs about intelligence and learning. Those who believe they can get smarter and understand that it takes effort and practice to get stronger with their skills are considered to have a "growth mindset." They tend to be more motivated to work harder, enjoy challenging lessons that help them learn more, and are interested in expanding their intelligence. They do not believe they have a single unchangeable level of intelligence, but rather that they can change and expand their intelligence over time, with practice. As a result, they are more likely to apply themselves, practice, and learn more, which results in them having expanded intelligence.

The alternative to growth mindset is fixed mindset. As you might expect, this type of mindset is the exact opposite to growth mindset. People who have a fixed mindset believe that they have a foundational or fixed level of intelligence that cannot be changed, no matter how hard they try. They are less likely to attempt to learn new things because they do not think they can, and they are put off by challenge. They prefer things to be easy and like to have everything done perfectly. People with a fixed mindset tend to think that even minor failures have a terrible reflection of who they are, and they can be extremely devastated by them. This may be why they gravitate towards doing things they are already good at and refrain from learning anything new.

Neuroscientific   Discoveries

 Recently, there have been neuroscientific discoveries that support Carol Dweck and her colleague's theory. Neuroscientists have learned that the brain is significantly more malleable than previously known and that there is a direct correlation between experiences and neuron connectivity. We know that when someone practices something new, existing neural networks grow new connections. They also strengthen existing ones and build insulation around the connections which are responsible for speeding up the transmission of impulses.

What this translates to in layman 's terms is that the more you practice something, the more your brain grows. Not only does it grow to accommodate for the new lessons and skills, but it also strengthens the existing ones. The more you practice new things, the healthier your brain's ability to develop new neural pathways is and therefore the easier it is for you to learn new things in the future.

There are specific "good habits" that can be practiced, which are responsible for helping to increase these neural pathways and strengthen the existing ones. Actions such as practicing, asking questions, and nourishing your body with healthy foods and adequate rest can all contribute to your ability to have a healthier brain that has a better growth mindset.

The Value of Growth Mindset
Alongside neuroscientific discoveries, many other researchers were beginning to understand more about growth mindset as well. They learned that there is a strong link between mindset and achievement. In other words, if you believe you can, you can. If you believe you cannot, you cannot. Those who believe they can learn new things, that their brain can grow, or that they can do any other number of things they desire often can. They find a way, and as a result, it happens. Alternatively, those who do not believe they can, do not. This is because they have a fixed mindset and

therefore a decreased level of motivation and achievements.

You can see that it is extremely important for people to invest in having a growth mindset so that they can successfully achieve anything they set out to do. Whether they want to increase their salaries, learn new skills, expand their brain capacity, or otherwise do something, those who have growth mindset will almost certainly be able to achieve it to some degree. Those who do not will never achieve what they desire to achieve in life.

When Does Growth Mindset Benefit You?

Growth mindset can benefit you in many numbers of situations. You can do virtually anything you set your mind out to do when you have a growth mindset. Simply based on the fact that you believe you can enable you to make things happen. You can learn to increase your financial wealth, learn new skills, learn new languages, expand your vocabulary, take up new hobbies, increase your physical well-being, increase your brain activity, and many other things when you adopt a growth mindset.

How Do You Get a Growth Mindset? Regardless of what type of mindset you presently have, fixed mindset or growth mindset, you can certainly transition so that you have a growth mindset. Learning to develop a growth mindset takes time and practice, but with the proper application of techniques, adequate time and patience, and enough effort, you can have a growth mindset. Throughout this book, you will learn exactly how you can establish a growth mindset for yourself, and how you can maintain it as well. That is exactly what this book is designed for!

Growth mindset is a powerful mindset state and strategy that will help you accomplish virtually anything you set out to do in your life. There are many people who benefit from their growth mindset, no matter what stage they were in their life when they developed one. Whether you have had a growth mindset all along, or you are learning to have one now in adulthood, you can still benefit from growth mindset. It is never too late to learn about the values of growth mindset, and how you can use it to expand your quality of life and lead your best life possible.

Chapter 22: Procrastination And Your

Brain

Procrastination and several biological conditions go hand in hand such as attention deficit disorder, executive dysfunction, anxiety disorders, sleep problems, stress and depression. The executive segment of your brain regulates, integrates and coordinates with the different systems and structures of your brain to give you a sense of yourself with your skills, values, goals and personality. Your inner executive draws information from your thoughts, history and senses. It then utilizes the information in a manner which directs you towards your goals.

Executive functions

A person who has a poor executive function would struggle with key life skills despite possessing several mental strengths.

When you remember that whatever you do today is linked to your future, you will be able to inhibit the urge to respond to your immediate desires.

You do not have to land into depression pondering about the future.

Depressive conditions make you feel less connected to life, less engaged and energized.

You would be less optimistic and motivated than usual.

Depression: Theme and variations

When you are sad, you do not care much about life and feel hopeless. You would not be careful in carrying out any task at work or personal front. You would not feel like mingling with your friends and you would not feel like caring for your body. If you feel depressed in life, you are probably procrastinating on important matters. You may suffer from seasonal affective disorder if the procrastination takes the form of feeling lethargic, sluggish and if you are unable to push yourself in going out during the winter months.

Obsessive compulsive disorder as well contributes to procrastination. When people with OCD are preparing a list of pros or cons, they are actually accomplishing nothing. They repeat behaviors and thoughts as their brains are stuck somewhere and the process is just iterating. You do not need to have OCD for experiencing brain lock. Procrastinators become paralyzed when they are really quite anxious about committing mistakes.

Most of us have more clutter in our life than we can take. However, some people procrastinate so much that their quality of life gets compromised in clearing it out. They find it difficult to make decisions about what to discard and what to keep.

Anxiety Disorders

Putting things off can prove to be stressful for many procrastinators. They worry that they have loads to do yet they do not do anything.

When they finally make up their mind to meet a deadline, they feel really stressed due to the last-minute stresses.

Chronic stress results due to chronic procrastination. This is neither good for your body nor for your brain.

The effects of stress

Stress magnified during procrastination.

It is more of a vicious circle. Stress produces procrastination and procrastination produces stress.

You have less creative energy available when your body is bearing the impacts of leading a stressful life.

This can hamper your creativity in doing things that you normally enjoy doing.

Sleep: Sleep debt & Sleep apnea

Your brain cannot function well if you are not sleeping well.

You would experience typical issues due to insufficient sleep such as inability to focus, irritability, low energy, low frustration tolerance and finally procrastination.

There would always be a biological component that you would experience no matter what your struggles with procrastination are.

Your brain perceives danger somewhere in the process of delays.

This is when procrastination offers protection and response.

Chapter 23: The Importance Of A Morning Ritual

So, why is a morning ritual all that important for you? Let's take a closer look at understanding the importance of the same, so that we can have a sense of knowing exactly how beneficial it can be for us, before we begin to work on that blueprint of the perfect morning ritual.

Why a morning ritual is so important for you

It triggers your subconscious mind

You will see that when you have a great morning ritual in place, your subconscious mind is automatically engineered towards designing the kind of life you strive to create; the life that you have always wanted but forever thought was out of your grasp. Thus, you don't have top always do things on a conscious level for the betterment of your world; they simply seem to happen on their own accord, even though it is you who are doing them out of habit.

It helps to set the tone for the day

You will see that whatever you do in the first few hours of the morning, will set the tone for the entire day to come. If for instance you start the day checking those emails on your phone, then you will be starting your day with a bucket load of anxiety. If on the other hand you choose to do something really constructive like going for a run, you will come to see that your mind is firmly anchored in the peaceful state it should be in – that very state that will continue for the rest of the day, simply because you have chosen to start your day with feelings of calm and positivity.

It gives you the much-needed reason to get out of bed in the first place!

You will find that when you are accost to staying in bed for longer than you should, you tend to get lethargic and that sense of lethargy will linger on for the rest of the day, as we have already come to understand in the preceding point. You will come to see that you are now able to get out of bed because you have a solid reason to – to indulge in that morning ritual which will not only make a difference in the day to come, but is something to relish in itself. You will feel the wonderful feelings of positivity that will serve as bait and ensure that you never have to press that snooze button again.

It helps to spark off your creativity

The one thing that sets us apart from other people out there is our own individual creativity, and when we have a good morning ritual in place we will come to see that you are far more inclined to be creative over the course of the day, thanks to that clarity of mind that you develop because of the highly successful habits you have inculcated over the course of the morning.

It helps give you that much needed 'me-time'

A lot of us are always complaining about how we don't have any time for ourselves. Well, if you start the day without giving a thought to what you really need, there's little chance that you will have any drive or energy at the end of the day to do the same. By doing those important things first thing in the morning, you will come to see that you can effectively have all the me-time you want, and at the same time not compromise on your work in any which way.

It gives you the much-needed momentum to do more in your workday

Think of that morning routine of yours as being a jump starter for the rest of your day. You will come to see that you can work far more efficiently than you ever could, simply because you have already set the ball rolling and gotten that jumpstart you needed to go through the rest of the day with an amazing sense of energy and a good deal of motivation. You will be able to get far more done in the course of the day, thanks to that all important momentum your morning ritual has provided you!

Chapter 24: What Is Productivity

Productivity is by definition an economical measure of output per unit of input. Inputs encompass work and capital, and output is measured in **profit**. It is the capacity to produce output from a given set of inputs.

The definition of productivity in business is: "a measure of worker efficiency, such as one hundred units per hour. In **economics**, it is involvement in the creation of **goods and services** to produce wealth"

Productivity is considered a key source of economic growth and benefit. I would say the key to success. It measures are a whole host of inputs calculated against a series of outputs.

Productivity measures can assist us to determine in which way we can maximize the use of the resources at our disposal, to the fullest extent and efficiency. That is the best way to higher achievements and revenues.

Our purpose in life is to succeed, to learn, and to progress. The only way to grow is to continually learn and accumulate knowledge in order to widen our mind and spirit. Learning and expanding my experiences is, in my opinion, the best thing to thrive and prosper in life.

Succeeding in life is dependent on how we test our experiences and how we choose to understand and to assimilate them, and how to respond to them. Our perspective and point of view can be crucial in our way to a better and more successful life.

The life depends on the way we make our choices. A succession of choices results in a whole rank of consequences. Every single choice we make has implications in the future which will generate a certain future event. So an appropriate choice will create an optimal outcome.

In other words, productivity is the efficiency with which, the economy as a whole, changes inputs which are all kind of resources like work, capital, services and raw materials, into output that can be for example, profit. Productivity increases when output grows faster than inputs, which leads to more productive and efficient inputs. Productivity—measures how efficiently we use our resources in order to produce.

As I said in the introduction, everyone has a personal definition of productivity:

An economist will say that productivity is the ratio of output to input and a company executive will be convinced that productivity is a gross value added, minus the lessening of the inputs used to achieve the production.

A technologist will say that productivity is to change improvident and wasteful performances, by improving the work systems, the technology, the equipment and the teamwork, but if you ask a simple laborer, he will say that productivity is how to get higher wages and better working conditions, with the same amount of labor investment.

The businessman will define productivity as finding methods to spend the minimum cost and earn maximum benefit.

A consumer will assume that productivity means to get more goods for a lower price, while an investor will try to obtain the best profit for his capital.

The best results we can obtain are characterized by good work, quickly and efficiently done, within the shortest time.

Productivity is the result of a multitude of factors:

-**motivation**

-talent

-training

-**environment**

-support from others

-time management

There are people seeming to be born multi-tasking, super-producers, but the majorities of us have to exercises and practice new ways, on a daily basis, to help us get things done.

Chapter 25: One And Two, This Is Your

Cue

Step One and Two on Overcoming Procrastination

Step One: Start Easy

You may think I am joking, right? Alas, I am not. Starting easy is the key to getting over procrastination. Pick the easiest thing on your list and get started doing that first. You will find when you do this, the momentum you gain while going from each task will rise exponentially. By the time you get to the rather large items on your list, you will be filled with so much energy that you are ready to take them head on.

The main reason someone procrastinates is that they get a sense of impending doom when they think about large assignments that need to be completed. Yes, that may sound rather out there, but that is what a person feels whenever they get stuck with a task that is far too long and complicated. They wait until the very

147

last minute before the begin working on it, knowing that they could make mistakes. That is when you make the most mistakes on a project is when you have to hurry to complete it.

Why not save yourself the time and errors, by utilizing this step in overcoming procrastination? Yes, we all loathe the idea of completing rather large tasks set in front of us, but we do not have another option. The tasks set before us are ultimately our doing; so why not go ahead and get them complete? It will save you time, and save yourself from having to edit it further if it turns out to be a written piece. You will be able to do an initial edit before the time to finishing it occurs, thus never having to see it again.

So, step one ... start easy. Let your momentum build with each thing you accomplish. It may seem daunting when you first begin, however, when you get into the swing of things it will be better. I can assure you, the feeling that is residing in your stomach. The bottomless pit of anxiety over this assignment will disappear if you have a system, and that system is starting easy. You will not be able to think about that particular task until you have finished all the others.

Step Two: Start Anywhere

This step goes along with step one. When you start easy, you may ask yourself where you should start, right? That's the thing; you can start anywhere. Take one of the small tasks, complete it, then keep working your way down the list until everything is finished. You may be scratching your head, asking yourself, "Is it really that easy?" I am here to tell you, yes. Yes, it is that easy. You are the only person that gets to choose what does and does not happen to you. If you do not deem it favorable, then you do not have to complete it.

However, that is not to say everything that comes your way is going to be favorable, either. There are a few things that you will need to take, even if you do not want to. It will broaden your horizon; make everything seem clearer for you. All you have to do is take that step. Take the initiative of completing something that diverse from what you are used to. Yes, it may seem hard at first, but once you get to that step, you will figure out how the rest of it goes. Show the determination that you can and will do anything you set your mind to. Do not let something so minuscule dictate who and what you are. Rise above it. Prosper. Set goals for yourself that you know will be difficult to reach, but not impossible.

You may find that you want to start on the challenging project first. If that is the case, then I suggest getting yourself hyped up as much as possible. It may lag your finishing time, but just the same, you will finish it. The main thing procrastination does is keep you from the things you need to accomplish. It gives you sense there is more time when there could be less. It makes you doubt yourself and your actions. The key to overcoming that is not allowing it to dictate who you are as a person. Do not enable it to cause you hardship. Thrust it out of your mind, get

150

down to work, and you will be able to accomplish anything you set your mind to.

Chapter 26: Understanding Habits

What you will learn here:
What are habits
What is dopamine, and why it's important
The three R's of habit formation
The "Five-second rule."
What are habits?
First of all, we need to define what a habit is. Habits are essentially a mechanism, with three major parts: the reward, the cue, and the routine. Our body developed this mechanism throughout our evolution: they are a routine of behavior that our mind wants to keep, because, in some way, it brings us benefits. By now you should be thinking "But eating fast food is a habit, and it isn't beneficial to our health!", and that is a fair point, perhaps to understand why fast food becomes a habit, you have to understand that fast food gives us an ejection of a hormone

called dopamine, and the brain loves dopamine, that is why bad habits are so difficult to break. Let's look at dopamine, as it is a fundamental part of habit formation, and it is essential to understand them.

Dopamine and its importance

Dopamine is what makes us feel good and energized, it is the reason why you like chocolate or any other food. Using food as an example, eating is one of our strongest habits because every time you eat something you like, there is a strong injection of dopamine in your brain, and you feel great for eating it; this feeling is what strengthens the habit of eating.

Dopamine is part of a mechanism that our brain uses, which rewards us every time we do something, it could be eating a certain food, drinking alcohol, hanging out with friends or even laughing from a pun. This mechanism evolved when humans were primitive and had little stimuli to motivate them, so the brain developed dopamine. This way, every time the human does something beneficial to their survival, the brain releases dopamine. Perhaps, in a society in which almost nothing is life or death related this mechanism gets over-used, and that is what causes vices, this includes playing videogames, smoking, eating junk food, watching pornography, social media, etc.

One of today's society's biggest problems is when something that our brain likes, for example, fat food, becomes easier to find than it used to be. So let's see why eating fast food becomes a habit: in primal times, fat food was really hard to find, as it was necessary to kill an animal to get it, because fat is one of our brains major fuels, the brain had to find a way to motivate humans to fight for it, and that is why a big dose of dopamine is released in our brain every time we consume fat, making us feel good while eating it. This is why fat food is so tasty, and why it is prone to become so addictive.

Macdonald's, Burger King, and other fast food chains built empires around our innate need for fat, and now fat is easy to find and when something that our brain really cherishes becomes easier to find than it was, it is always telling us to get more and more, because in primal times, we never knew when it would disappear, leading us to want more and more. This is how vices are created. This is a habit that is really hard to fight because our brain wants us to continue it... this is a bad habit.

Dopamine is a key factor in habit forming, perhaps, there is actually a cycle for each habit. There are three factors that make up the habit, also known as the 3 R's of the habit. They are what you should target to break or make a habit.

The cue (trigger or reminder), the reward and the routine.

Here is a visual demonstration:

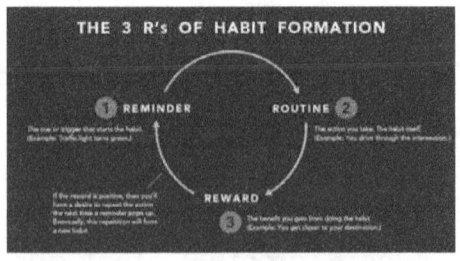

Triggers or Cues

Our brain needs something to tell it that it is time to perform the action, and that is called a cue or trigger. This cue can be anything; it could be a time of the day, or someone arriving home, between other things.

For example: Let's look at Richard. Richard has been eating fast-food at lunch for 10 years, and he now wants to stop eating junk food, perhaps he can't. Because when it comes to midday, he just gets an urge to eat a hamburger. In this case, the trigger is the time of the day. To look at another example let's see Barry. Barry and his brother used to play videogames every day, all day. Barry now wants to stop playing videogames, but every time he sees his brother near him, suddenly a need to play video games start to rise inside of him, and he can't think about anything else for the rest of the day. In the first example, the cue was the time of the day, while in the second one, it was Barry's brother. It's important to remember that the cue can be anything.

Basically, it is the trigger that reminds the brain about the habit and that you need to perform it. This is called classical conditioning in psychology, you may have smoked with that person so many times before that now you are conditioned to smoke every time you see them, or maybe you ate fast food at lunch so many times before that now you have to eat it every time lunch hour arrives.

Reward

The reward is what makes the habit stronger. If the reward is positive, the habit strengthens, if it is negative, the habit weakens.

Now don't think that these rewards are your normal definition of rewards, once again, you have to think from the perspective of someone who lived in the primal times. Rewards are usually psychological needs, instead of physical. Things, like socializing, day-dreaming, or making yourself feel useful to others, are some examples. This is really important, because most people think that the rewards they need are consumable, but in fact, we humans can leave fairly well without these. This misconception happens primarily because advertising and marketing made their way into our lives and corrupted our innate sense of "reward."

There are times when you think that you want something, perhaps you actually want another, for example, Anthony thinks he wants an ice-cream, but he might just want to get up from his desk and day dream a little bit, or he may want to eat something, which doesn't have to be an ice-cream or he might want to see someone who normally is in the place he goes to get ice-cream and socialize a little bit. This is really important because you need to find the reason why you want that ice-cream, as that will empower you to change that habit. To find out what the reward is, you should do the following: if your habit is getting up to eat a donut at your office's bar, then one day get up and, instead of going to the bar, take a walk and allow yourself to daydream a bit. Next day get up, go to the bar and socialize, but don't eat anything, the other day, buy something healthy to eat.

Check if any of these ideas made you feel satisfied. Find your reward. To do this, you can write on a piece of paper the first five words that come to your mind, this way you will know what is in your head.

The Routine

This is the simplest out of the three. The routine is the habit, as it is what you usually perform. In the part about the cues, I said that "you may have smoked with that person so many times before that now you are conditioned to smoke every time" and that is your routine. You had the routine of smoking with that person or eating fast food at lunch, so it developed the habit of doing it. The brain picks up your routine and says: Well, since he has been doing this so many times, and it brings so much pleasure, it must be a good thing! Maybe I should pick it and make it permanent so that I don't have to remember to do all of this every day. And so the brain automates all the process behind your routine and makes it a habit so that you don't need to think about it every time you perform it.

The Circle of Habits

As you can understand it is possible to see a pattern here: The cue remembers the brain about the habit which makes you enter in the routine, which leads you to do the action that provides you the reward. If the reward is positive, it reinforces the cue and the circle restarts. Let's look at an example: John is very bad at communicating with other people, this is due to his habit of saying "humm" in the middle of his phrases. This happens when he forgets about a word or runs out of things to say about a subject. This is the cue "running out of things to say or forgetting a word". The reward is hearing himself saying something out loud, even if he can't remember the word he wants to say. The routine is saying "hummm" when he can't remember a word. You can think about this cycle as a plant that is growing inside of you, every time you water it, it grows stronger in you. Using this analogy, it is possible to say that certain habits have developed so much that if they were plants, their roots would be really intricate within you, so much that getting rid of them is almost impossible. After all, this said, it is up to you to grow nice trees that help you develop and grow, or to grow weeds that suck all the time, energy and space in your life. It is up to you to decide whether you want to nurture good habits or bad ones.

Craving

When the bad habit becomes really ingrained in you, a fourth step rises, the craving.

This happens when your brain wants to perform the bad habit. Wanting to bite your nails is an example of a bad habit that developed a craving.

This is why it is common to say that when you wake up in the morning craving a drink, you are an alcoolic, because the craving only surges when the habit is formed and automatized.

Changing your habits is at the end of the day your decision. This book can only help you so far. I want you to think well about it, and figure out if you are really dedicated to change your habits and ultimately your life.

To summarize:

Habits are repetitions of behavior that make that behavior simpler because they are always being reviewed.

Habits are made of three major parts: cue, reward, and routine.

The cue is what remembers the brain about the habit.

The reward is what strengthens the habit. If the reward is positive, the habit becomes stronger, if it is negative, the habit weakens.

The routine is essentially the habit.

Productivity tip: Everybody knows that motivation comes and goes, and there is no shame in admitting it, especially when you are doing things that go against what your brain wants for you. However this is no excuse since everyone has to do things they don't like, but still, you shouldn't trust only on your willpower to do all the little things that being successful requests. Knowing this, I decided to give you a helping hand in the form of a rule, the five seconds rule.

The Five seconds rule:

Nobody is made of iron, and we all know that so it is well known to everyone that some days you are on your high road and others you are down, and it's when you are down that it can be difficult to sustain your objectives, mostly due to the fact that, if you are doing things out of your comfort zone, your brain is programmed to make you not to maintain your habits. Moments when you stop a little to think about what you are doing, and you start to hear that little voice inside your head that says to you "why do this?", "I can't do that, that is impossible for me!", "Just push the sneeze button, you can sleep for five more minutes, it's okay.", "Eat that slice of cake; you deserve it, come on.". These moments sometimes happen 4-5 times a day, and most of the time when you don't possess counter measures against them, you will fall for them, and all your progress will be wasted. So what should you do? First of all, don't panic, this just means your brain is healthy, this is its function, to keep in your comfort zone. In fact, this is your limbic lobe talking, while you actually want your frontal lobe to be in control because that is the part of your brain which can think long-term about your life.

This is the part of the brain that can tell you not to eat that slice of cake because it starts with just one, but one slice a day here, another there and when you notice you have fallen victim of that bad habit again. To activate it, you can do one thing very simple: **Count from 1 to 5 backward.** Very simple yet so powerful. Count from one to five backward and then do what you are supposed to do. You can do this early in the morning to get up from the bed, or to calm yourself down, the possibilities are endless, I know I use it every day, and it has helped me a lot.

If you want to know more about it, I would recommend you check the work from Mel Robbins, as she was the one who showed me this rule, through her book.

At the end of the day, it isn't important how you do it, only that you keep yourself focused and never give up from what you setup to do. If you give up, then you will never see progress. To get the extra motivation, I always like to check biographies and stories from successful people when they were struggling, because that just shows everyone is the same and that we all have rough moments. Just don't forget that we have all been there. If you don't give up, better days will come for sure.

Chapter 27: Identify Your Time-Wasting

Habits

Would you be able to tell someone, off the bat, what time you wake up and go to bed? Can you state exactly how many hours you are awake each day? Can you pinpoint the specific times throughout the day when you are productive and when you are taking breaks?

If you are having trouble figuring out exactly how you spend your time each day, then you may have a problem with managing your time effectively. This is a common problem, particularly in the digital age where people get easily distracted by an explosion of information from the internet, particularly in the form of social media and video games. To manage your time effectively, you should first know the daily habits that are keeping you from doing so. Here are the steps:

Establish your goals.

The first step is to determine how you want to spend your time each day, and you can determine this by knowing your goals. Ensure that the goals are detailed and concrete, and that you have a specified deadline for each of them.

For instance, if one of your goals is to take the final exams three months from now, then it means you may want to spend a specific amount of time each day reviewing. Once you have established your goals, the next step is to determine how you can make them fit into your daily schedule.

Take note of how you usually spend your day.

Establishing a daily schedule will require you to know how you spend your day first. Get a piece of paper and a pen, then reflect on what you usually do as soon as you get up in the morning. Then, continue jotting down the activities you do all the way until you go to bed at night.

If you cannot seem to retrace your steps this way, what you can do is to keep a daily journal for at least a week. In your journal, make a record of what time you got up each day and what time you went to bed. Also, create a bullet point list of the activities that you did that day.

Here is an example of what a one-day entry may look like:

-Woke up at 7:45 a.m.

-Ate breakfast, took a shower, got ready for work

-Left for work at 8:50 a.m.

-Came in 15 minutes late, worked on report. Spent time on Facebook and Twitter.   Answered emails. Chatted by the cooler with Irene and Amanda.

-Lunch at the caféat 12:30 p.m.

-Worked on report and surfed the internet.

-Went home at 5:15 p.m.

-Watched television series while surfing the internet on the phone until 8:30 p.m.

-Ate microwave dinner while chatting on Facebook.

-Took a shower, brushed teeth, surfed the internet. Watched YouTube videos.

 Watched a movie on Netflix.

-Went to bed at about 1:15 a.m.

If how you spend your weekends is different from your weekdays, you can create separate lists for them as well. Some people would even have different lists for each day of the week, especially if they work freelance.

Highlight your time-wasting habits.

Once you've gotten a grasp of how you spend your time each day, the next step is to identify the habits that keep you from being productive each day. One way of doing that is to highlight these time-wasting habits on the list (or lists) you have made.

In the example above, it could be that the person is spending too much time online and going to bed late.

You can identify whether a certain habit is bad or good by comparing it with the goals you have set. If these everyday habits serve no purpose to your long-term goals, then you can easily label them as time wasters.

After identifying your time-wasting habits, you can then resolve to overcome them. The succeeding strategies will provide you with plenty of tips on how to do that.

Chapter 28: Overcome Procrastination

Take Action on What You Avoid

The first step to overcome procrastination is to identify the parts of your working routine that are stopping you from staying on task. If are able to identify what is eating away your time and attention then you will know where to start making changes.

Everybody lingers here and there, yet 20 percent of individuals stray away from difficult or uninteresting chores and purposely search for distractions as a way of getting out of the task at hand. Procrastination is commonly caused by lack of self-control and willpower. "I don't feel like it" is an excuse that may seem innocent at the time then next thing you know you have fallen down a rabbit hole of wasted time and creating last minute stress that could have been avoided.

Procrastinators may state they perform better under pressure, yet as a general rule the added pressure of limited time and resources usually results in work that is only a fraction of the quality in which they are capable of producing. The beautiful side? It's completely possible to defeat procrastination—with exertion. Perfectionists are regularly procrastinators; it is mentally more satisfying never to handle an assignment than to face the fact that your work has fallen short of your expectations.

The mental inceptions of procrastination – and how we can quit putting things off

"I love due dates," English creator Douglas Adams once wrote. "I love the whooshing noise they make as they pass by."

We've all had the experience of needing to complete a project, however, putting them off for some other time. At times we do this because we couldn't care less about the venture, yet when we find ourselves in different circumstances we care a lot– and still, end up accomplishing something else. I, for one, ended up cleaning my home when I have a considerable amount of papers to review, despite the fact that I know I have to review them I still made the decision to clean my home instead.

So why do we linger? I think it's safe to say that we have all found ourselves in this situation at some point in our lives, so why do we let ourselves reach that point instead of learning our lesson? Maybe one of the main reasons we become trapped in this cycle is because of how we view our work and the routine surrounding it?

These questions are vital to my exploration on objective interest, which could offer a few pieces of information from neuroscience regarding why we hesitate – and how to beat this bad habit.

To do, or not to do

Everything begins with a straightforward decision between working now on a given task and doing something else: chipping away at the other project, accomplishing something fun or doing nothing at all may just seem like a more appealing choice at the time but is likely to set you back later on.

The choice to chip away at something is driven by the amount of drive you feel towards finishing the project at that time – what analysts call this is subjective value. Furthermore, procrastination, in mental terms, is the thing that happens when the benefit of accomplishing something else exceeds the benefit of working at this point.

Along these lines of intuition proposes a straightforward trick to stopping procrastination in its tracks: figure out how to increase the benefit of working now, outweigh any . You could build the evaluation of the project, diminish the estimation of the diversion, or some blend of the two.

For instance, rather than cleaning my home, I may attempt to concentrate on why grading is personally vital to me. Or, on the other hand, I could consider how unpalatable cleaning can be – particularly when sharing a house with a little child.

It's straightforward counsel, yet holding fast to this technique can be tough, basically because there are such a variety of strengths that reduce the benefit of working in the present.

The inaccessible deadline

Individuals are not by any means reasonable in the way they feel things. For instance, a dollar bank note is worth the same today as it is seven days from now. However, its subjective value – generally how great it would feel to possess a dollar – relies on upon different elements other than its face value, for example, when we get it.

The tendency for individuals to devalue cash and various merchandise in light of time is called delay discounting. For instance, one review demonstrated that, on the whole, accepting $100 three months from now is justified to be same to individuals as getting $83 at this moment. Individuals would preferably lose $17 then hold up a couple of months to get a bigger reward.

Different elements additionally impact subjective value, for example, how much cash somebody has as of late gained or lost. The key point is that there is not an immaculate match between objective esteem and subjective esteem.

Delay discounting is a calculate procrastination because the finishing of the venture occurs later on. Completing something is a delayed reward, so its value in the present is decreased: the further away the due date is, the less alluring it appears to deal with the venture at this moment.

Studies have more than once demonstrated that the tendency to procrastinate intently takes after economic models of delay discounting. Moreover, individuals who portray themselves as procrastinators demonstrate an exaggerated impact. They discount the benefit of completing something early significantly more than other people.

One approach to expanding the benefit of finishing an undertaking is to make the end goal appear to be nearer. For instance, simply envisioning a future reward diminishes delay reducing.

No work is "easy."

Not exclusively can finishing a project be depreciated because it occurs later on, yet working on a project can likewise be unpleasant because of the underlying certainty that work requires energy.

New research underpins the possibility that mental effort is naturally expensive; therefore, individuals work on a less demanding errand as opposed to a harder assignment. Moreover, there are more noteworthy subjective expenses for work that feels more difficult (however these costs can be offset by involvement with the job needing to be done).

This prompts the intriguing expectation that individuals would procrastinate progressively the harder they anticipate that the work will be. That is on account of the more effort an errand requires, the more somebody stands to gain up by putting a similar measure of exertion into something else (a marvel economists call opportunity costs). Opportunity costs make taking a shot at something that appears to be hard feels like a loss.

Beyond any doubt enough, a gathering of studies demonstrates that individuals procrastinate more on unpleasant assignments. These outcomes recommend that lessening the agony of taking a shot at a project, for instance by breaking it into more familiar and manageable pieces, would be a powerful approach to diminish procrastination.

Your work, your character

`When we compose that procrastination is a reaction to the way we value things, it outlines task completion as a result of inspiration, as opposed to ability.

As such, you can be okay at something, regardless of whether it's cooking a gourmet dinner or composing a story, yet if you don't have the inspiration, or feeling of significance, to finish the undertaking, it'll likely be put off.

It was thus that the author Robert Hanks, in a current paper for the London Review of Books, depicted procrastination as "a failure of appetites."

The wellspring of this "appetite" can be somewhat precarious. However, one could contend that similar to our (genuine) hunger for food; it's something that is nearly interwoven with our day to day lives, our way of life and our feeling of our identity.

So how can one expand the subjective value of a project? An intelligent way – is to interface the venture to your self-idea. Our theory is that projects seen as imperative to a man's self-idea will hold more subjective value for that individual.

It's therefore that Hanks likewise composed that procrastination appears to originate from an inability to "distinguish adequately with your future self" – at the end of the day, the self for whom the objective is applicable.

Since individuals are spurred to keep up a positive self-idea, goals associated nearly to one's feeling of self or character go up against a great deal more esteem.

Interfacing the venture to more immediate wellsprings of value, such as life goals or core values, can fill the shortage in subjective value that underlies procrastination.

Chapter 29: What Is Procrastination

Merriam-Webster defines procrastination as the act or habit of intentionally putting off something that should be done.

As early as this point, it is important to differentiate procrastination from resting. We recharge when we rest. Rest is necessary as it enables productivity. In fact, proper time management incorporates periods of rest.

By contrast, procrastination is delaying, needless, and counterproductive (Schraw, Wadkins, Olafson, 2007). In a sense, what distinguishes required rest from procrastination is planning and prioritization.

On the other hand, workaholism is not necessarily the opposite of procrastination. Sometimes, a workaholic exerts too much effort in the office but procrastinates in other aspects of life, using work as a scapegoat perhaps.

At the end of the day, we just have to honestly answer the question: Should I be doing something else at this moment that I'm consciously not doing, even though I can actually attend to it right here and right now?

If your answer is yes, you are most likely in the zone of procrastination.

Scope and Effects of Procrastination

Procrastination can span different aspects of life: household chores, health and fitness, school work, office work, relationship (building or mending), career, finances, personal goals and dreams, and even spiritual pursuits.

When procrastinating, a person does certain activities that rationalizes the behavior. These coping or defense mechanisms can be classified into 3 main groups.

Please refer to the chart below:

Avoidance and Denial	- Avoiding the person, place, or situation - Denying that behavior is procrastination - Denying that delayed task is urgent or important,

	trivializing - Just being lazy or lazing around and not focusing on task at hand
Distraction	- Distracting self in other tasks - Celebrating achievement in the task used to procrastinate
Emotional Maneuvering	- Blaming external factors for delaying (person, task difficulty, situation) - Gloating or smugly comparing self with others who had it worse (procrastinated but got a C, not failing like classmate) - Mocking or using humor to criticize people who work too hard

At its most basic, procrastination results to cramming, missed deadlines, and loss of productivity. But it can also affect a person socially: poor relationships, disapproval and punishment due to delays, poor social image, and social stigma.

Physically, it can result to poor quality of life such as stress, lack of sleep, and diseases that could have been prevented if not for delaying seeking medical advice and treatment.

It can also lead to poor emotional and psychological health, as chronic procrastination may lead to feelings of inadequacy, guilt, helplessness, self-doubt, and even depression. Over time, these negative feelings might end up to having poor self-image, as being helpless and inadequate, and under-achieving and not realizing potential.

Process of Procrastination and Anti-Procrastination

Like any other forces of habit, procrastination is a thought that becomes a choice and an action. When a person chooses to procrastinate again and again, it eventually becomes a way of thinking and a way of living.

thought → choice → action → repetition
→ way of thinking → way of living

The good news is that you can always stop procrastination at any point in this process, as long as you are willing to change. You can actually use this same process to stop procrastination in its track and reverse the cycle.

The first step is *awareness*: awareness that you have succumbed to procrastination before, and perhaps it is luring you again at this point in time.

The second step is *choice*: being open to the possibility of doing the alternative to procrastination, which is getting things done now.

The third step is *action*: just do it now.

The last steps are on *repetition*: do it over and over again until it becomes automatic to you.

Awareness and choice can happen in a snap. Maybe you have reached your tipping point when you just say, enough of this procrastination. Action may take long, depending on the nature of your task, especially if it requires preparation.

Repetition takes longer, but do not stress yourself about this yet. Take it one step at a time, and watch how your small choices and actions add up.

Before heading into detailed how's, let us first examine the why's. Knowing yourself and understanding your underlying reasons for procrastination can help you in choosing tools and methods that are tailor-fit and aligned to your situation, personality, and temperament.

Chapter 30: Changing Your Mindset

In order to make some changes in your life, in this case changing your habits ties to laziness and procrastination, you must first resolve a problem that started it all: you need to change your mindset and start thinking differently. By changing your perception of how things are, you will be able to accept all the new changes coming in your way and making your life far better and procrastination free.

Hack #1: Acknowledge

You should first start with acknowledging that you do have a problem with laziness. Basically, you have already started usi8ng hack #1 even before you read this sentence as you have bought thins guide and decided that it is time to get rid of bad habits that come hand in hand with procrastination. By acknowledging that the problem does exist, you are making the first step towards resolving your problem. Just admit it to yourself: I have a problem with laziness and everything else seems to be better and more important than things I am actually supposed to be doing. There you go! You have mastered hack number one, so now you can move onto more serious stuff, getting closer to completing your goal of getting rid of procrastination with each hack you go through with.

Hack #2: Prioritize

No matter how lazy you may be at times or constantly, falling into long episodes of procrastination where you can do nothing constructive or work on something that actually matters, you surely know your priorities. If not, you should settle your priorities down and decide what is of the most importance to you. Here is the first task for you: make sure you don't avoid doing it, finding a better amusement! It's not hard actually, as the only thing you need to do is take a piece of paper and write down every task you have to do for today, writing them from number 1 to number n, making number one the most important thing you need to do for today. You can also have that list written down for all the things you need to do during a week or during a month, making those your long term tasks set by priorities. Priorities are made up by importance of things you need to do, so if you have something work related, naturally you will need to do that first then move onto tasks that have less importance or less urgency attached to them.

Hack #3: Determination

Well, hack number 2 might as well fall into a river and drown if there isn't for hack number 3: you need to be determined that curing procrastination is just the thing you want to do. Now, procrastination is not an illness, but it is still a very bad habit that is making you postpone fulfillment of your dreams and goals by having you easily distracted with things that are trivial and not as important as it takes you nowhere in your life. We all have that one day when we just want to set back and relax, doing nothing productive, but it's just ONE day in a week, making a couple of days in a month. You can still enjoy your free time after you have finished everything you are supposed to do. That way enjoying your free time at the end of the day will come as even more enjoyable, knowing that you have made one heck of a productive day. All you need is determination.

Hack #4: Consequences

This hack will be sort of your electro shock. Anything you do has consequences, which might remind you of you Physics class in high school: Each action has an equal or opposite reaction. That been said, even if you do not make any action, in this case not doing the tasks that are supposed to be completed, you are actually doing something: procrastinating. And that action has an equal reaction, meaning that there will be consequences for everything you do or do not do. So, you will use this as a constant reminder that will come as sort of a warning, which will help you push yourself into stop being lazy. You can think about it this way: if you finish your tasks on time, you will get a reward. Reward in this case can be solely a sense of accomplishment, but the reward can also be material. Let's say that you have a deadline for completing work-related task. If you don't complete it on time, but instead choose to procrastinate always finding something "better" or more interesting to do, there will be negative consequences. You can get fired or disciplined or reproached, etc. If you have, however, do your work on time, there will be positive consequences as you might get rewarded ort praised, feeling accomplished and responsible, which is a great feeling. You should definitely try it. Use consequence awareness as you constant reminder that there will be reaction to your action or the lack of your action.

Hack #5: Consistency

In order to achieve diminishing all signs of procrastination, you need to be consistent with your decision to do so. That means that you will have to practice each and every day with being productive, starting with smaller steps and motivating yourself into succeeding in doing so. Being consistent is very important because that way you are also practicing good habits of being productive and completing your tasks on time. Make yourself into solving at least one task per day, gradually increasing the number of tasks you will work on, on daily basis. That way you will develop a habit. You can choose a certain time of the day that is reserved for being productive and try and stick to that time, doing nothing but working on the task you have given to yourself.

Hack #6: Motivation

Motivation always works the best even if there is something waiting to be done and we don't feel like doing it. Motivation of finishing work related tasks is easily visible: money. If you don't do your job within the given deadline and within your assignment, you won't get paid and that means that you won't be able to afford food, rent, bills and all other necessary things you most certainly need. But, finding motivation for cleaning your house or even achieving your long term goals can be a bit tough. You can live in a messy house with not a single clean dish if it's up to you, and your goals can be postponed to be worked on tomorrow that will never come. However, you will feel the consequences of postponing, as you will eventually realize that some things can't wait forever to be resolved. To make finding motivation easier for you, you can use the same motivation for everything you need to do and that motivation can be the feeling of achievement that feels great as it encourages production of serotonin, hormone of happiness, and who doesn't like to be happy, right? So, whenever you feel like not doing something that you are supposed to, just imagine the way you will feel after you are done. You will feel fulfilled, contempt and proud of yourself, which is maybe the best kind of motivation you can possibly get – all other positive consequences that might come as positive "side effects" would be an additional plus that will show you that being productive really pays off.

Chapter 31: Using Microsoft Outlook

Microsoft Outlook is a **great software to use as a to-do list** especially if you are in a company with few employees, or if you are a freelancer or maybe working on small projects.

It helps you manage activities easily with the simple features that allow you to create simple to-do lists, set reminders and track time easily.

Why should you use Microsoft Outlook?

One of the benefits to using outlook for your tasks is that it **has a quick way of converting emails into tasks**, especially if your outlook is connected to your main email.

You simply drag the email to the preferred section of the list depending on the urgency. This is a fantastic feature because many tasks are received by email this day.

By converting the emails to tasks, you easily control your email and spend less time looking at activities in your email.

Also, **for security reasons**, you are required to use an approved software. You do not want your tasks or activities to leak, exposing them to the third party.

Therefore **outlook as a safe software** to use since your tasks are stored safely in the outlook internal servers.

How do you use outlook to-do list?

If you are using the recent versions of the outlook, then you can **use the task list in the to-do bar**.

You will, however, **have to make several changes** to fit the to-do list that we discussed in the second chapter (with the three urgency sections).

You can follow these steps to make the changes.

Look for the task list in the to-do bar located to the right of your screen

Right-click the arranged by (or arrange by) label at the top of the task list.

Remember to keep tasks in each section as brief as possible.

Also, keep an eye on the tasks regularly depending on the urgency as seen in chapter six.

You can always change the section depending on the activities you have.

Chapter 32: What Is Procrastination?

To understand what's causing you to procrastinate you need to know what it truly is. There's no "one cause" for procrastination which is why it can be so hard to tackle or even tell when you're doing it. Sometimes time gets away from us and suddenly we've not done the things we set out to do at the beginning of the day.

The Lingo

The term *procrastination*, was originated from Latin word, *procrastinatus,* which itself originated from the prefix *'pro-',* which means *"forward,"* and *'crastinus,'* which means *"of tomorrow."* Procrastination could best be defined as delaying, deferring, and putting off the task to a later time. Sometimes tasks can be put off, and by putting them off you learn new things and can tackle them better than before. It is only when procrastination starts to hinder us from having a full, active life that it becomes alarming.

You might be procrastinating at doing your work, or maybe at home with house chores.

It is common to hear statements like these from a procrastinator: "I will do this later" or "I am more motivated to work under pressure." However, there is a greater possibility for a procrastinator to put off things indefinitely or even use the procrastination as a way of getting out of the task entirely. Can you even count the time's someone you know decided that "tomorrow, I will start my diet" only for them to eat terribly the next day and put it off again?

Where it comes from

It's generally believed that we learn to procrastinate. Procrastination could be learned from parents, siblings, or anyone who surround as we grow up who make us understand that it's okay to put things off.

For the majority of people we don't actively choose to procrastinate.

Subconscious

Procrastination is controlled mostly by the left side of the brain which is responsible for reasoning and analytical thinking. The Ego part of our psyche also dwells in the left hemisphere and this part is responsible for both our personal identity and perception of reality. Our Ego determines the emotional response and perception needed to cause us to act.

Part of what makes procrastination hard is that you're fighting your own psyche. Inside you probably tell yourself "it will never happen" or "you'll fail anyway" so you simply don't try. By creating that belief that the action is impossible your brain releases similar chemicals to those experienced when you're in pain. Since you're trained not to enjoy pain the brain chooses to put that action into short term memory where it can be quickly recycled and forgotten and we can be happy again. We don't even realize we're forgetting to do it.

Faulty Programming

Sometimes, procrastination is a reaction to a strict parenting style. Having parents who are controlling may keep kids from developing the capability to take instant action without looking for some extra guidance from a role model in their life. There are cases where procrastination may be a form of revolt or even a means to just seek attention from parents who hover over their child.

The way we are "wired" is often determined by out parents but it's also determined by out routine. We all have routines that we follow to get jobs done. Take mornings – for some people they're awake as soon as their alarm goes off, while others have to slowly zombie shuffle for a little then inhale coffee and "awaken". People who are not morning people force themselves to get up and be productive because they have to. Whatever reason they are awake has a higher priority than that of sleep.

Personally, I'm productive in the mornings and late at night but during the day I tend to meander a lot. This is important, because I know when I get things done. When are you most productive or most likely to complete a task?

What we do is we prioritize – we determine how quickly a task can be completed based on our perception of its value. This wiring is important because it determines what we do and don't accomplish. But we're not always correct in our perceptions and while our brain thinks we're prioritizing and getting stuff done, we're actually just choosing to put them off with good intentions.

Another reason your brain might be wired to procrastinate is that you think you're a procrastinator. Many times we label ourselves as something and accept it, so we follow that behavior. IF you believe you're a procrastinator then it's more likely you will procrastinate.

Addicted to Procrastination

It's also possible to be addicted to procrastination. Sometimes we consciously procrastinate, knowing we will get the task done at the last minute or because by leaving things to the last minute we have somehow managed to do something spectacular in the nick of time. Consider someone who arrives late to an event, their entry will be noticed, so they make themselves late because they crave the attention it will give them. You create your own excuses or your own reasons because you know that by putting off a task you are choosing to do you'll be "noticed" when you do complete it.

Another way you can be addicted to procrastination is the push of getting things done at the last minute. Consciously leaving things to the last minute (because we don't get whatever perceived reward we're getting until after that last minute) means we equate the worth of the task only high enough when the actual reward is at hand. You leave a project finished until the last minute because until then the deadline is far away and completing it will not release the same brain rewarding chemicals until the deadline passes. I am extremely guilty of this. I often leave things until deadline knowing I will push hard to get them done because it's that race to the finish line that excites my psyche because the reward isn't the same when it's been done for weeks and I have to wait.

Procrastination comes in a lot of different forms. You might know it's important for you to finish a certain task, but then you'll find millions of ways to avoid it. How you procrastinate is key to figuring out how to stop yourself doing it so that when you look at those long-unfinished tasks at the bottom of your to-do list you won't feel disappointed in yourself.

Conclusion

Fixing your procrastination is going to be hard at first, but eventually, it gets easier because you build better and more successful habits. In the beginning, you will need to fight fiercely to cling to your habits and attain your goals. During those first days, take your chance to learn from your struggles and mistakes. They are going to make you stronger, and they're going to teach you what to look for in the future to keep you successful.

How could you be less narrow-minded about your indefinable tasks?

It is essential to prevent procrastination from overtaking your life. Every time you have to make a decision and execute the right actions against procrastination, it is going to be that much easier to do the same thing again in the future. By following the steps mentioned above, you will find a way to create the right habits that work for you and your method of procrastination.

If you're a perfectionist, like I was before, deep down you know that human nature is imperfect. I know, the saying that goes "nobody is perfect" may sound cliché, but it's a fact and is something you have to keep in mind all the time. You will fail, there will be times you procrastinate, but one thing is for sure, the more you try, the more successful you are likely to become.

The moment you achieve success, and you've prospered and reached your selected goals, give yourself credit as well! You overcome procrastination!

Thank you for reading this book. If the information in here was in some way helpful for you go ahead and leave a review, it will be very much appreciated. I've endeavored to get my thoughts down in such a way that you can understand them. However, procrastination is a very personal problem and you'll need to find your own habits and strategies to figure out what works best for you.

Good luck and I hope you reach your goals.

9 781989 965016